STAMPEDE FOR GOLD

THE STORY OF THE KLONDIKE RUSH

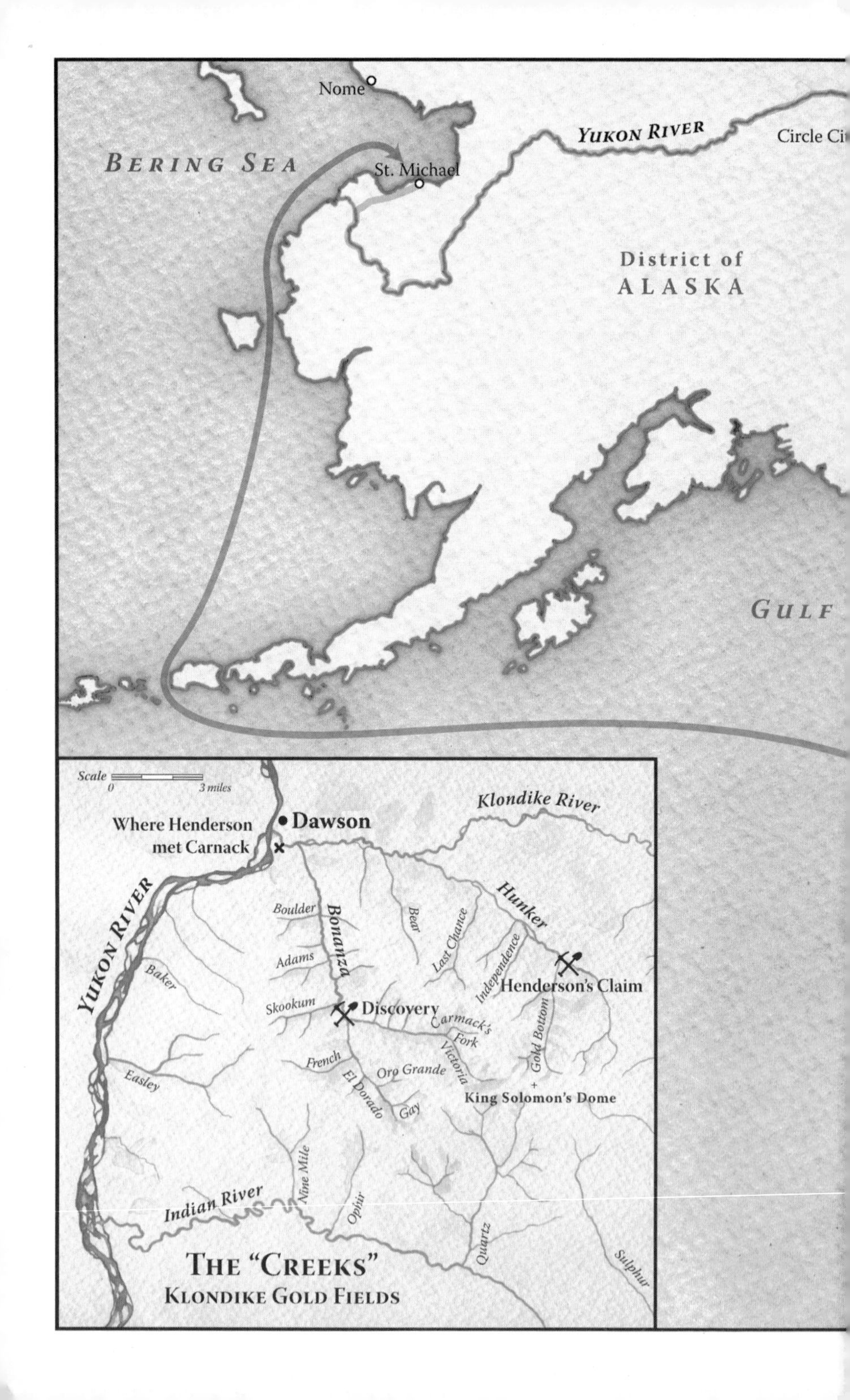

Nome
BERING SEA
YUKON RIVER
Circle Ci
St. Michael
District of
ALASKA
GULF
Scale
0
3 miles
Klondike River
Dawson
Where Henderson
met Carnack
YUKON RIVER
Boulder
Bonanza
Bear
Last Chance
Hunker
Independence
Adams
Baker
Henderson's Claim
Skookum
Discovery
Carmack's
Fork
Victoria
Gold Bottom
French
Oro Grande
El Dorado
Gay
Easley
King Solomon's Dome
Nine Mile
Indian River
Ophir
Quartz
Sulphur
THE "CREEKS"
KLONDIKE GOLD FIELDS

YUKON
Territory
Fortymile
Dawson
Inset map, lower left
Pelly River
Yukon River
Whitehorse
From Edmonton
CANADA
Inset map, upper right
Skagway
Lake Atlin
Juneau
LASKA
BRITISH COLUMBIA
ROUTES NORTH
"Rich Man's Route"
"Poor Man's Route"
"All-Canada Route"
Vancouver
Seattle
From San Francisco
PACIFIC OCEAN
BENNETT LAKE
Homan Lake
Bennett
Scale
0
5 miles
Lindemans Lake
Lindeman City
Log Cabin
Happy Camp
Crater Lake
Fraser
The Scales
Chilkoot Pass
3,739 ft
Sheep Camp
White Pass,
2,890 ft
Mt. Cleveland
6,350 ft
Canyon City
Mt. Carmack
6,605 ft
White Pass City
Finnigan's Point
UNITED STATES
CANADA
Goat Lake
Dyea
Taiya Inlet
Skagway
THE PASSES

Klondike Stampede, 1897
Miners crowding Porcupine Hill along the White Pass Trail to the Klondike region of Yukon Territory, Canada.

STAMPEDE FOR GOLD

THE STORY OF THE KLONDIKE RUSH

PIERRE BERTON

New York / London
www.sterlingpublishing.com/kids

To my Father

who was there

A FLYING POINT PRESS BOOK

Design: PlutoMedia and John T. Perry III
Frontispiece: The Granger Collection
Front cover painting: John Berkey for the United States Postal Service © 1998

Library of Congress Cataloging in Publication Data

Berton, Pierre, 1920–2004.
Stampede for gold : the story of the Klondike Rush / Pierre Berton.
p. cm. — (Sterling point books)
Includes index.
ISBN-13: 978-1-4027-5121-9
ISBN-10: 1-4027-5121-4
1. Klondike River Valley (Yukon)—Gold discoveries—Juvenile literature.
2. Frontier and pioneer life—Yukon—Klondike River Valley—Juvenile literature.
3. Pioneers—Yukon—Klondike River Valley—History—19th century—Juvenile literature. 4. Gold miners—Yukon—Klondike River Valley—History—
19th century—Juvenile literature. I. Title.

F1095.K5B47 2007
971.9'101—dc22 2007013356

2 4 6 8 10 9 7 5 3 1

Published by Sterling Publishing Co., Inc.
387 Park Avenue South, New York, NY 10016
Originally published in 1954 by The Macmillan Company of Canada under the title
The Golden Trail: The Story of the Klondike Rush
Published in 1955 by Alfred A. Knopf under the title
Stampede for Gold: The Story of the Klondike Rush

Distributed in the United Kingdom by GMC Distribution Services
Castle Place, 166 High Street, Lewes, East Sussex, England BN7 1XU
Distributed in Australia by Capricorn Link (Australia) Pty. Ltd.
P.O. Box 704, Windsor, NSW 2756, Australia

Printed in China

Sterling ISBN-13: 978-1-4027-5121-9
ISBN-10: 1-4027-5121-4

For information about custom editions, special sales, premium and corporate purchases, please contact
Sterling Special Sales Department at 800-805-5489 or specialsales@sterlingpub.com.

CONTENTS

Author's Note ix
Before . . . 1
1 The Luck of Siwash George 17
2 Millions in a Moose Pasture 31
3 The Richest Poor Men in the World 44
4 The Great Rush Begins 56
5 Three Thousand Dying Horses 68
6 Starvation! Flee for Your Lives! 74
7 The Terrible Chilkoot Pass 83
8 A Thousand Trails Led North 97
9 The Great Armada Down the Yukon 109
10 Stampede's End 120
After . . . 140
Index 155
About the Author 165

AUTHOR'S NOTE

THIS STORY OF ONE OF HISTORY'S STRANGEST mass movements is as faithful an account as the author can make it on the events as they occurred between 1896 and 1899. Nothing has been invented and nothing has been fictionalized. Conversations and dialogue where they occur are reproduced as reported by people who were there, either in interviews with the author, in diaries, or in published reports.

STAMPEDE FOR GOLD

THE STORY OF THE KLONDIKE RUSH

BEFORE . . .

IN THE WINTER OF 1885–86, MORE THAN TEN years before the discovery of Klondike gold, a dying prospector came out of the dark, unknown Yukon country. His name was Williams and he had performed a feat that was considered impossible. With an Indian boy he had traveled by dog team up six hundred miles of frozen Yukon River. Then he had climbed up over the terrible Chilkoot Pass to reach a tiny trading-post on the seacoast where the Alaska Panhandle begins.

The man and the boy had suffered fearful privations. The weather was so bad that all the dogs had died of cold and fatigue. At the top of the pass they had been trapped by a blizzard. Here they had crouched for ten days in a hastily built snow house, existing on dry flour. Williams could no longer walk. The little boy carried him four miles down the mountain slopes. Then he pulled him on a toboggan the remaining twelve miles to the seacoast.

The two of them staggered into John Healy's trading-post, and here Williams died. The handful of men at Dyea crowded around to look at the dead man. No one had ever before walked out of the Yukon in winter. What, they asked, would bring a man on such a harsh journey? The Indian boy had the answer. He reached into a sack of beans on the counter, took out a handful, and flung them on the floor.

"Gold!" he said. "All same like this."

With these dramatic words, the outside world began to learn that there were riches in the Canadian Yukon and in Alaska, which lies next door to it. There had been only a few scattered reports before this. Ever since the discovery of hardrock gold at Juneau, on the Alaska coastline, adventurous men had been trickling in twos and threes into the mysterious, silent country to the north. Some of them had found fine gold in the sandbars of the Yukon and Stewart rivers. But this new discovery on a little creek called Fortymile was the first real strike.

At that time there were only about two hundred white men living in the whole vast region of Alaska and the Yukon. These two enormous territories cover more space than California, Oregon, Washington, Montana, Idaho, Wyoming, and Nevada put together. They are bisected by the swift, broad Yukon River. It flows in an enormous semicircle for twenty-two hundred miles, starting near the Chilkoot Pass and arching northward over the Arctic Circle and back down again to the Bering Sea. It was the country's only highway. Most of the Alaska-Yukon towns lay along its shores.

Fortymile was the first of these towns. It lay just inside the Yukon border, a thin line of log cabins straggling along the riverbank. In these days of airplanes it's a little hard to realize just how isolated it was. Living in Fortymile was very like living on a desert island.

There were only two ways to reach the town. One way was to go by boat, six thousand miles from Seattle. The boat went right around the coast of Alaska to St. Michael on the Bering Sea near the mouth of the Yukon River. Here you transferred to a tiny paddlewheel steamer. It took you fifteen hundred miles upriver to Fortymile.

The other way to reach Fortymile was to take a coastal steamer to Dyea, Alaska. From here you climbed over the pass, built your own boat on the other side, and floated downriver about six hundred miles.

Fortymile was so far from the sea that the paddlewheel steamer could make only one or two trips each summer. This boat was the only source of supply for the town. One year it didn't reach Fortymile. So two hundred miners had to leave at once on foot for the outside world. Otherwise they would have starved.

For these reasons Fortymile was a primitive settlement. Everything had to be brought thousands of miles into the country, usually on men's backs. There was no window glass in Fortymile, for example. Various things were used as substitutes. Sometimes untanned deerhide was tacked across the small hole in the cabin wall. More usually the tiny gap was plugged with a row of empty bottles or pickle jars.

There was no furniture as we know it. Stools were made from blocks of trees. Tables and beds were simply beams strung between the logs of the cabin wall and a couple of uprights. Tableware was made of tin. Often enough four men would live in a cabin just sixteen feet broad and eighteen feet long.

The staple diet in the camp was bacon, beans, and tea, and occasionally moose meat. It's hard to imagine how the Yukon could have been settled without beans. It was difficult, in those days, for a man to resist the cold climate without their wonderful heating powers. They would be cooked in batches and devoured cold or perhaps slightly warmed on the trail.

Flour was another staple. It was used to make sourdough pancakes and biscuits. And it was from this yeast substitute—sourdough—that the old-timers derived their famous nickname of Old Sourdoughs. A tin of sourdough—literally fermented dough—hung over every stove. A little of it would raise a fine batch of biscuits.

There was no paper or silver money in Fortymile. All business was transacted in gold dust. Every miner carried a poke—a little bag made of tanned moosehide. When he wanted to buy a drink in one of Fortymile's log-cabin saloons, he handed his poke to the bartender, who measured out a quantity of dust. It was a firm custom that a customer always turned his back when the dust was being weighed out on the scales. It was considered a gross insult to watch the bartender, for that cast a slur on his honesty. And honesty was the rule in the Yukon gold camps. The most terrible crime of all was theft, for theft from a man's cache of supplies might mean death by starvation.

There was another custom in Fortymile that all abided by. Every man left his cabin door unlocked. If a stranger passed by, he was welcome to come in whether the owner was there or not. He could feed himself and bed down for the night, but he was duty-bound to clean up after himself and leave a stock of freshly split wood behind.

These customs had the effect of laws and they were there for mutual protection. An open cabin might save a man's life in a storm or cold snap. A lack of fresh kindling or firewood might cause his death from cold. Indeed, life in the Yukon was run on a co-operative plan. If a man didn't find enough gold to keep him for the winter, he was allowed to go out to the diggings and pan enough to buy a year's outfit. Similarly, the Alaska Commercial Company extended almost unlimited credit to those prospectors who needed it. The company had to do this. You couldn't let a man starve in the dead of winter simply because he was without funds.

Fortymile was never a very rich camp. In fact, its population was made up of poor laborers who, within a few years, were to become Klondike millionaires. But in those days the Klondike was only a salmon stream about fifty miles upriver. It would have been hard to convince any Fortymiler that under the moss and the devil's clubs lay more than two hundred million dollars in gold dust and nuggets.

Although Fortymile was situated on Canadian soil, it was really an American town. Its population was almost entirely American. Its supplies came from the United States, from San Francisco or Seattle. It celebrated the Fourth of July and Washington's Birthday. There wasn't a custom's man the entire length of the Yukon River, and this Canadian town boasted an American post office selling American stamps. Later on, when the famous Northwest Mounted Police arrived in 1894, the situation changed somewhat. But the atmosphere was never completely British.

Fortymile was never the lawless, blood-and-thunder settlement that some of the towns in the American west were. Most of the miners were educated men with a taste for literature. They made their own entertainment. There were, for example, regular debating societies and Shakespeare clubs where miners took the roles of various characters in play-readings. Books on science and philosophy were widely sought. Some men wrote poetry. And there was a curious organization known as The Forty Liars. This was a group of men who lived on an island in the Yukon River, a mile or two above town, called Liars Island. They spent their time telling tall stories.

The Anglican Church in Fortymile was well attended. This was largely due to the presence of Bishop William Bompas. He was an Englishman with the face of a hawk and a huge flowing white beard. He had spent a quarter of a century in the north. The previous minister in Fortymile had gone insane because the miners played so many practical jokes on him. But Bishop Bompas was cast in a stronger mold. His diet was hard and his wants were few. His bed was a hole in the snow, a corner of a boat, or a bunk in a cabin. He allowed himself no holidays. When he finally built some furniture for his mission house, he had to tear it apart again to make a coffin for a dead Indian.

Bishop Bompas became a respected figure in Fortymile as he sat in his cabin, reading his Bible in English, Greek, Hebrew, and Syriac (for he spoke all these languages), while his wife, a cultured Englishwoman, sat beside him, reading Dante in Italian. A strange background for the son of one of England's most eminent advocates, this dark, silent town on the banks of the Yukon!

But, nine years after gold was found at Fortymile, an even stranger town came into being on the banks of the Yukon River, some three hundred miles downstream. This was Circle City, the largest log town in the world. Like Fortymile, it was a gold town.

The gold had first been discovered by one of Bishop Bompas's colleagues, an Archdeacon MacDonald. He was a missionary who had spent most of his life with the Loucheaux Indians, far to the north. He picked up a few nuggets in a spoon one day and threw them aside. Months later he casually mentioned the fact that he had found gold on a creek somewhere near the Arctic Circle. Archdeacon MacDonald was interested in souls, not in gold. But for years men talked about the mysterious "Preacher's Creek," where nuggets lay on the sands to be picked up by the spoonful. Then two Russian half-breeds found the creek. When the word leaked out, most of the population of Fortymile rushed downriver to start a new town.

Circle City was aptly named. Not only did it lie close to the Arctic Circle, but it also lay at the head of the great Yukon flats. This is a huge prehistoric lake bed where the river spreads out over the surrounding countryside until it is several miles wide.

And at the point where Circle City lies, it describes a great circle.

Birch Creek, where the gold lay—the legendary "Preacher's Creek"—was about seventy miles from Circle City. To get to the mines you had to take a trail across a marshy plateau full of shallow ponds and stunted spruce. Here in the wet muskeg the mosquitoes were so thick that in June and July they often blacked out the sun. Men from Circle City sometimes went raving mad because of these mosquitoes. Game, which was easy to find elsewhere, shunned this no-man's land. No man could move across it unless every square inch of his body was covered. Horses had to be swathed in canvas sheets. Their nostrils had to be cleaned of insects every few minutes to keep them from suffocating. But the four hundred residents of Circle City made the trip regularly because of the gold.

Surely this was one of the strangest towns in the world! It had no taxes, no courthouse, no jail, no post office, no church, no school, no hotel, no dog pound. It had no sheriff, no police, no mayor or council. It had no written law. It had no dentist, doctor, lawyer, or priest. It had practically no crime, and there wasn't a lock in town. There wasn't a single piece of dressed lumber in town either. Everything was made of log.

It was a silent city. Only the occasional howl of a dog broke the stillness. In the winter there was so little movement that the smoke drifted straight up from the cabins and hung over the town like a dark blanket. The chief recreation was gambling, the smallest coin in town was a dollar, and the saloons gave unlimited credit. As usual in Yukon and Alaska camps, the residents were often cultured men. One was an Oxford graduate. His wife was an Indian woman who had taken to bleaching her hair in order to appear Caucasian. Another man used to quote classical Greek every time he had a few drinks. All these people left one another strictly alone, and a man could do pretty much as he wanted in Circle City as long as he minded his own business.

There was, for example, one man called Johnson who tried to commit suicide by cutting his throat. His friends stood around silently watching him. He made a bad job of it, so they bandaged him up and left him. When he came to his senses, they told him cheerfully that if he wished to try again he was welcome to. But Johnson had had enough. He grew an enormous black beard to hide the scar. This, plus his new nickname of Cutthroat Johnson, frightened those tenderfeet who didn't know his background.

Circle City's leading citizen was a trader named Napoleon LeRoy McQuesten. Nobody bothered with all these names, for up and down the river he was known simply as Jack. He was the most respected man in the Yukon and continued to be until he died in 1911. He was a huge, bluff man with a great blond mustache, and they called him, correctly, the Father of the Yukon.

Jack McQuesten had been a frontiersman in the Oregon Indian wars and a sailor before the mast. He had spent twenty-five years up and down the Yukon River, trading with the Indians. His partner, a wiry little steamboatman named Al Mayo, had started life as a circus acrobat. It was McQuesten and Mayo who had founded most of the trading-posts along the Yukon, and it was McQuesten who had established Circle City.

McQuesten's first trading-post had been Fort Reliance, just six miles from the mouth of the Klondike River. He had often shot moose up the famous creek later to be named Bonanza. But of course Jack McQuesten never thought of looking for gold in a moose pasture.

McQuesten traded on commission for the Alaska Commercial, the pioneer trading company of the Yukon and Alaska. He extended unlimited credit to all, for he trusted every man. And because every man trusted him he lost very little by this policy. One day a miner came into his post at Circle City and asked McQuesten how much he owed him. The bill came to seven hundred dollars.

"Seven hundred?" said the miner. "Gee, Jack, I've only got five hundred. How'm I goin' to pay seven hundred with five?"

"Oh, that's all right," McQuesten said. "Give us five hundred and we'll credit you and let the rest stand until next clean-up."

"But, Jack," the miner said, "I want my stuff. How'm I goin' to get it?"

"We'll let you have it same as we did before," said McQuesten.

"But, Jack—I haven't been on a spree yet."

"Well," said the trader, "go and have your little spree and come back with what's left and we'll credit you with it and go on as before."

But when the miner returned there was nothing left. McQuesten gave him his outfit anyway.

McQuesten was responsible for inventing Circle City's first thermometer. He put a set of glass vials in a rack. The first one contained quicksilver. The second contained whisky. The third contained kerosene. The fourth contained a cure-all known as Perry Davis Painkiller. They congealed in the order mentioned as the weather grew colder. When the Painkiller turned to slush, no one set a foot outside his cabin door.

McQuesten was also the central figure in a curious annual ceremony. On a given day in the summer all the women in town would collect together with a blanket made of sewed mooseskins. In this they would toss every white man in town. After each man was tossed in the air, he would throw food or tobacco into the skin. McQuesten was always honored by being tossed first. But before the tossing took place the big trader would be allowed to escape. Then, when he was encircled, a fight would take place until he was conquered. No matter how high he was tossed, he always landed on his feet. Not until 1896, when he was fifty years old, did he fall on his back. Then all the women gathered around and patted him sympathetically.

It was in McQuesten's store, or in one of the saloons, that the curious gatherings known as miners' meetings were held. These constituted the only courts of law that Circle City knew. They were meetings of all the citizens, held to settle all disputes or to punish the occasional crime. The chairman of the meeting acted as judge. A clerk was appointed to take minutes. The plaintiff stated his case and produced witnesses. The defendant replied and produced more witnesses. Anyone present could ask a question and anyone could stand up and discuss the case. At the end of the discussion the entire meeting voted on the verdict and the majority ruled.

One famous miners' meeting gave a verdict on a suit for breach of promise. A saloonkeeper had broken his promise to marry a mixed-race girl. The girl's cousin called a miners' meeting and the whole town turned out for it. Even the six white women in town were invited, for this was an affair of the heart. The saloonkeeper was found guilty and given two choices: he could pay a fine of six hundred dollars and marry the girl, or he could pay a fine of five thousand dollars, spend a year in jail, and not marry her. As there was no jail in town, the meeting decided to build one if needed. But to everybody's relief the guilty man took the first course. As in most cases, the fine was spent on the spot—in the saloon.

There was one murder case in Circle City. It involved another saloonkeeper named Jim Kronstadt and a miner named Jim Washburn. Washburn had a reputation for bad temper, especially when he drank. One day, after a heavy drinking bout, he roared down the street chasing a little miner named Archie Burns. With Washburn brandishing a pistol and bent on murder, Burns ducked into Kronstadt's saloon. The saloonkeeper was standing in front of the big pot-bellied stove with his hands clasped behind his back. He didn't see Burns duck in and squat down behind the stove. A moment later Washburn entered and demanded to know where Burns was. Kronstadt, taken by surprise, said he didn't know. Washburn roared that he was lying.

"I'm going to shoot somebody. It might as well be you," he shouted.

Kronstadt realized he meant it. He thought his last moment had come. Then, to his astonishment, he felt a gun, ready cocked, being slipped into his hands, which were still clasped behind him. Kronstadt whipped the gun upward and shot his opponent dead between the eyes. Then he posted a notice calling a miners' meeting to try himself for murder. The meeting speedily found him not guilty, on grounds of self-defense. The verdict was forwarded to Washington, D.C., and the acquittal was upheld there. Thus the miners' meeting was given the force of a court of law.

But it was theft, not murder, that caused the most serious miners' meetings. The seriousness of this crime may be gathered from the following sign in the dining room at Twelve Mile Cache on the Birch Creek diggings:

TO WHOM IT MAY CONCERN

At a general meeting of miners held in Circle City it was the unanimous verdict that all thieving and stealing should be punished by whipping at the post and banishment from the country. The severity of the whipping and the guilt of the accused to be determined by the jury. So all thieves beware.

The theft that met with the severest penalty in these pre-Klondike days involved a Circle City man who robbed a cache. A cache is a small log hut on stilts. Here the miners kept their winter's provisions safe from marauding animals. Because of the isolation a man could easily starve if his cache was robbed.

Circle City was particularly incensed by a man who robbed a cache and, after taking what he wanted, threw the rest on the ground to spoil. He was found guilty at a miners' meeting, and the sentence was death by hanging. But because the miners were a little uneasy at carrying out the death sentence, he was given an alternative. He could, if he wished, take a hand sled without dogs and leave for the Outside—a journey of more than a thousand miles on foot, in the dead of winter, through mountainous unpopulated country.

In effect, this too was a sentence of death. On the day of the guilty man's departure the entire town came down to the riverbank, shook hands with him, and wished him luck. Then they stood and watched him disappear around the big curve in the river. He was last heard of 375 miles upriver. From then on, no further word came from the man who stole from the cache.

And that's how it was in the Yukon and Alaska, in the days before the Klondike Gold Rush turned a silent empty country into a madhouse. And what changed it all?

The story begins with a man named Robert Henderson. . . .

CHAPTER 1

THE LUCK OF SIWASH GEORGE

ON A BRIGHT AUGUST DAY IN 1896, A TALL, rangy prospector came floating down the broad Yukon River in a poling-boat. His name was Robert Henderson, and ever since his childhood he had been looking for gold. Although he did not know it, he was now approaching the climactic moment of his life, an encounter which he would bitterly regret for the rest of his days.

Around the bend in the yellow-gray river lay the mouth of a fast, shallow stream which the Indians called Thronduick. On the banks of the stream lived a man named George Washington Carmack. He and a group of Indians were drying salmon, for at that time the Thronduick, or "Klondike" as it was sometimes called, was known as the best salmon stream in the Yukon.

It was this chance meeting between Bob Henderson and George Carmack that was to touch off one of history's strangest mass movements, the Klondike Gold Rush. Within a year the results of their encounter would electrify the world. A million men and women all over the globe would be fired with a determination to go to the Klondike. One hundred thousand would actually leave their homes. Forty thousand would eventually arrive on the banks of the salmon stream. Some would die here. Others would become wealthy. Carmack himself would be rich enough to throw nuggets by the handful from the windows of a Seattle hotel. But for Robert Henderson there would remain only the bitter memory of this bitter August day.

It was gold that brought Henderson down the river. All his life he had sought it. As a boy in Pictou County, Nova Scotia, he used to make excursions around the islands looking for nuggets. At the age of fourteen he sat down to think about it more seriously. As a result he determined to devote his life to a search for gold. He was convinced it lay in the southern hemisphere, so he signed aboard a sailing ship and for seven years he roamed the world. He found no gold, but he continued his roamings—up through the western badlands of the United

States to Colorado and thence north to Alaska and the Canadian Yukon.

Henderson had been unlucky in his search. Discouraged, he decided to leave the country and head back to Colorado. On the way back up the Yukon he stopped in at Sixtymile River, where a smiling French-Canadian trader named Joseph Ladue had his post.

If there had been a Chamber of Commerce in those days, Joe Ladue would have been president. He was a booster. He had spent fifteen years in the Yukon, trading up and down the river, and wherever he went he boosted that part of the country in which he traded. At the moment he was boosting the Indian River country not far from his post. He told everybody who came by that there was plenty of gold up the Indian River, which lay just over the divide from the Klondike. He did this because he knew that the more men who went up the Indian, the more would trade with him.

Few listened to Ladue. Everybody was convinced there was no gold up the Indian. It was on the wrong side of the Yukon, for one thing; everybody knew the gold lay along the creeks on the other side. It was in the upper river country, for another; all big discoveries had been made farther downriver. Its valleys were too broad, for a third; everybody knew the gold lay in the narrower valleys.

As it turned out, everybody was wrong. Millions of dollars in gold dust lay hidden in the Indian River country, but even Joe Ladue would have been surprised to hear it.

When Henderson arrived at Ladue's post he had just ten cents left in his pocket. He listened to the trader's optimistic stories and then turned to him and said, seriously: "Look. I'm a determined man. I won't starve. Let me prospect for you. If it's good for me, it's good for you." Ladue was happy to accept the offer. He outfitted Henderson and wished him luck.

Bob Henderson spent almost two years in the Indian River country, prospecting up and down the creeks and occasionally finding a little gold. All this time he was looking curiously up at the sharp mountain divide that separates the Indian from the Klondike watershed. Henderson was a restless man, and his eyes were always wandering to the hills beyond. What lay in the unknown country on the other side?

Finally, one day Henderson and three companions climbed to the top of the divide and looked about them. They stood on a dome-like mountaintop, and below them they could see the little valleys stretching off into the distance in various directions like the spokes of a wheel. Close to them was a little gorge, and the four men started down it through the tangle of underbrush. After a quarter of a mile of hard travel they stopped and began to prospect, dipping their pans into the gravel of the stream bed and swirling them around to see if any gold was left behind.

To their surprise, there *was* gold. The dull greenish little particles in the pan averaged about eight cents. This was not fabulous, but in those pre-Klondike days it was considered worthwhile. Before the brief summer was over, Henderson and his partners had taken seven hundred and fifty dollars from the little creek. Henderson decided to name it Gold Bottom because, as he said wistfully: “I had a daydream that when I got my shaft down to bedrock, it might be like the streets of the New Jerusalem.” Alas, it was only a daydream.

Late in July Henderson headed back over the mountain and down the Indian River for Joe Ladue’s post to get more supplies. The last stretch, up the Yukon, was slow, hard slogging, for the prospector had to pole his boat against the force of the current. But he was a strong man and used to hard work.

At Ladue’s he found a dozen prospectors. At once Henderson told them of his good fortune. It was a rule of the Yukon Order of Pioneers, to which Henderson belonged, that a prospector making a strike should spread the news to everyone he met. As soon as Henderson broke the news, all the men at the Ladue trading-post, including Ladue himself, headed toward the scene.

Henderson followed them back down the river. The water

was so low in the Indian, when he reached it, that he decided to take his boat up the deeper Klondike instead. Thus, in early August he approached the mouth of the salmon stream and his fateful meeting with George Carmack.

As he rounded the bend in the river, at the point where the Klondike roars out to mingle with the muddy waters of the Yukon, Henderson could see Carmack up on the bank with his two Indian brothers-in-law, Skookum Jim and Tagish Charley. In the background was Kate Carmack, the strapping daughter of an Indian chief, whom Carmack had married. The air was pungent with the smell of freshly cut spruce boughs and of salmon smoking over the fires.

"There's a poor devil who hasn't struck it," Henderson thought to himself. "I'll tell him of my good luck."

He brought his boat to the shore, climbed up the bank, and greeted Carmack.

They were a strangely contrasting pair, these two men who are jointly credited with the discovery of Klondike gold. Henderson was a lean, gaunt man with piercing eyes, a hawk-like face, and a thick, ragged mustache. Carmack was stockier, with heavy jowls, close-set eyes, and a drooping Oriental mustache such as the Indians, with whom he traveled, wore. These Indians were known as Siwash or Stick Indians, and Carmack was known throughout the country as Siwash George or Stick George. He was always rather pleased when someone would say to him: "George, you're getting every day more like a Siwash," for he liked the Indians.

Nobody in the Yukon took Carmack very seriously. He was known as a braggart and a boaster. Some of the miners called him Lying George because he occasionally came to Fortymile to announce that he'd struck it rich, though it was obvious that he hadn't. The nickname was a little cruel. It wasn't so much that George Carmack was a liar; it was simply that he was an optimist.

If Carmack and Henderson had one quality in common, it was the quality—or curse, perhaps—of restlessness. Like Henderson, Carmack was a wanderer, as his father had been before him. The elder Carmack had crossed the American plains in an oxcart during the California Gold Rush of 1849. Young George left home to be a sailor, drifted north on a windjammer, jumped ship at Dyea on the Alaskan Panhandle, and made his way to the Yukon country by climbing the snow-swept Chilkoot Pass and drifting down the river with the Indians. He had been eleven years in the Yukon, trapping, fishing, hunting, trading, and occasionally prospecting—all with very little success.

He was something of a mystic. In his cabin during the long winter nights he wrote flowery poetry. He depended to some extent on dreams and omens. In the spring of this same year he had left his cabin on the upper Yukon and flipped a coin to see whether he should go upriver or downriver. When the coin came down tails, Carmack loaded his boat and drifted down to Fortymile. Here he had a strange dream: he saw a swift stream full of grayling and two very large King salmon whose scales were made of gold nuggets and whose eyes were twenty-dollar gold pieces. Carmack interpreted this to mean that he should go salmon-fishing, and that was why Henderson found him living in a skin tent and smoking fish on the banks of the Klondike.

In the accepted tradition of the Order of Pioneers, Henderson told Carmack of his discovery on Gold Bottom Creek and invited him to come along and stake a claim. Carmack replied that he'd be glad to and added that he'd bring the Indians along as well.

Henderson frowned at this suggestion. It may be that his next sentence cost him a fortune. He muttered something about not wanting to stake the whole Siwash tribe. This remark rankled with Carmack and his relatives.

"What's matter dat white man?" Skookum Jim asked in the pidgin jargon of his kind, after Henderson had left. "Him killem Inchem moose, Inchem caribou, ketchet gold Inchen country, no liket Inchen staket claim, wha for, no good!"

Carmack had told Henderson that he would follow along in a day or so, and the next morning he and the two Indians set out. Instead of traveling up the Klondike to the point where

Gold Bottom joins it, they struck up another wide valley known as Rabbit Creek. Henderson's gold talk had made them curious, so they prospected as they went. At several points along this creek they found gold in small quantities—as much as ten cents to the pan. Then they turned up a fork in the creek toward Gold Bottom and climbed to the top of the same round bald hill from which Bob Henderson had got his first glimpse of the Klondike Valley.

It was a brilliant day. Below them the valley lay spread out like a rich Persian carpet. Streams rushed in torrents down the hillside, widening out into valleys which snaked off toward the Klondike River on one side and the Indian River on the other. In the distance the crimson and purple hills stretched off into the haze. On the horizon the snowcapped Rockies jutted up. In the foreground the huckleberry and salmonberry bushes formed a bright tangle.

Just below them was a small canyon from which rose a wisp of pale-blue smoke.

"Well, boys," said Carmack, "let's go down and see what they've got."

Henderson and his partners had dug out a deep gash in the frozen ground in order to reach the gravelly bedrock where placer gold is found in the greatest quantities. They invited Carmack to test out a few pans, and Carmack did so. He was not impressed with the results, for he felt that he had found equally good prospects on Rabbit Creek. Besides, the Indians were uneasy about Henderson. They asked him for some tobacco and offered to pay for it, but he refused to let them have any. The three men decided to head back over the hills again.

Henderson agreed that Carmack should prospect Rabbit Creek, and he asked him to be sure to let him know at once if he found any good prospects there. He suggested that Carmack send an Indian back with the message and offered to pay for the trip. Carmack promised he would, but this promise was soon forgotten. For this breach of faith Henderson was always to blame the other man bitterly. Carmack, on the other hand, never quite forgave Henderson for his attitude toward the Indians.

Back up over the hills the three men struggled, floundering over fallen logs and through spiky clumps of devil's clubs and tangled underbrush. Then down the other side they went until they reached a swampy flat dotted with great clumps of matted grass grown up over the decades. These served as unwieldy, treacherous steppingstones across the hip-deep muck of the glacial swamp. Soon their moccasins and trousers were soaking-wet and their faces burning from mosquito bites.

Finally they reached the head of Rabbit Creek and began to

follow it down to the general area where they had first found the gold. As they walked down, they came to a fork in the creek, and here they stopped for a moment to rest among the birches. They could not know it then, but at this point they were standing on the richest ground in the world. Underneath the thick blanket of moss lay millions upon millions in gold. Gold was all around them, even in the low benchland that rose above them. Here, in two years' time, would spring up the town of Grand Forks, a roaring, bustling center for eight thousand miners. Huge dredges are still churning up the creek and its fork and taking gold out of the gravels. As for the hills, they have long since been torn to pieces by hydraulic nozzles.

The trio walked on for about a quarter of a mile and then made camp. And here, at the foot of a birch tree on the edge of the stream, one of them found a bright nugget of gold. Who found it? We shall probably never know. Both Carmack and Skookum Jim claimed the honor. The Indian said he found it by accident after he shot a moose and was drinking in the stream. Carmack said *he* found it by design, after noting a strip of bedrock jutting out along the rim of the bank.

At any rate, the gold was there—raw gold lying thick between the flaky slabs of rock, like cheese in a sandwich. All three began to shovel the shale rock into a pan and swirl it around. They set the pan down after the gravel was washed away, and there lay a quarter of an ounce of fine gold. Here in this single pan was four dollars in dust, by far the largest amount ever taken from one pan in the Yukon up to that time.

The three men stared silently at the gold for several moments, and then suddenly they all began to do a war dance around the pan. It was, as Carmack said later, a combination Scotch hornpipe, Indian fox-trot, syncopated Irish jig, and Siwash hula-hula. Finally they sat down, exhausted, and washed out some more gold—enough to fill an empty shotgun cartridge.

They camped across the creek from their discovery that night. They were tired and hungry but filled with elation. Around the campfire they sat, smoking their pipes and staring into the coals. Suddenly the two Indians began to chant a wild, eerie song of praise to the Great Spirit. Carmack remained silent, alone with his thoughts. After eleven hard years in the north he was on the verge of unbelievable riches.

The next day they staked four claims. Each claim by law extended five hundred feet down the valley and extended across the creek from rimrock to rimrock. Carmack claimed discovery and was thus permitted two claims. Carmack staked *Discovery* and *One Below;* Skookum Jim staked *One Above;* Tagish Charley staked *Two Below.* From then on all future claims would be numbered from this point, above and below the *Discovery* claim. This was the seventeenth of August, a day still celebrated throughout the Yukon as the anniversary of the discovery of Klondike gold.

The three men shouldered their packs and set off for the mouth of the Klondike. On the way downriver they met four discouraged men wading slowly upstream towing a loaded boat behind them. These men, like almost everybody else in the country, had been drifting about on a fruitless search for gold. They had heard about Henderson's discovery on Gold Bottom and were looking for it. They asked Carmack if he knew anything about it.

"I left there three days ago," Carmack told them.

"What do you think about it?"

"Well, I don't like to be a knocker, but I don't think much of it and I wouldn't advise you to go up there."

The men's faces fell: after this long, hard journey, another wild-goose chase.

But Carmack hadn't finished. A slow grin spread across his face as he pulled the cartridge full of gold from his pocket.

"I've got something better for you," he said, and told them of his discovery. The men's expressions changed. They seized the ropes of their boat and started off up the river toward Rabbit Creek at top speed.

And so the elated Carmack moved down the river to the mouth, occasionally meeting other lonely, discouraged men and telling them of his good fortune.

"I felt," he said later, "as if I had just dealt myself a royal flush in the game of life and the whole world was a jackpot."

But there was one man he did not tell. On the other side of the divide, oblivious to the excitement on Rabbit Creek, Robert Henderson still toiled away, getting eight cents to the pan and never knowing that just over the hill the man he had invited to look for gold had discovered the richest ground in the world.

CHAPTER 2

MILLIONS IN A MOOSE PASTURE

GEORGE CARMACK AND TAGISH CHARLEY WERE floating down the Yukon River to Fortymile. Skookum Jim had taken a saw and an ax and gone back to Rabbit Creek to cut some wood and guard the claims. Along the creek, other men were already driving their stakes into the black muck and dreaming of undreamed-of riches. These were mainly men who had heard of Henderson's Gold Bottom discovery but who had been diverted by the news of Carmack's strike. There were not more than two dozen of them. From this small trickle, the Klondike Gold Rush stemmed.

Carmack walked into Bill McPhee's saloon in Fortymile. It was crowded with miners who had come into town from their claims to arrange a winter's grubstake. Carmack was not a drinking man, but on this occasion he ordered two whiskies to celebrate his good fortune. Then he told his story.

"Boys, I've got some good news to tell you. There's a big strike up the river."

"Strike!" said a bystander derisively. "That ain't no news. That's just a scheme of Ladue's to start a stampede."

Carmack tried to tell his story of the discovery, but he was greeted with jeers. The Fortymilers had heard this sort of talk from him before.

Nettled, he pulled the cartridge from his pocket and poured the gold onto the container, known as a "blower," near the gold scales on the bar.

"Well, how does that look to you, eh?" Carmack shouted.

The men crowded around.

"Is that some of the Miller Creek gold that Ladue gave you?" somebody asked.

But it was obviously not from Miller Creek or any other known creek in the Yukon. Alluvial gold takes different forms, and experienced men could look at a sample and quickly tell where it came from. This flaky gold, mixed with black sand, looked different from anything the men had yet seen. An uneasy feeling rippled around the bar. Could Lying George be telling the truth?

The following day, Carmack crossed the Fortymile River and recorded the four claims at the Mounted Police post there.

Then he headed back upriver. Before the day was out, most of the population of Fortymile had decided to follow behind him. Men slipped away in twos and threes at night. In a few days the town was deserted.

At the base of the hills, where the Klondike joins the Yukon, across from the spot where Carmack and the Indians had smoked their fish, lay a strip of frozen swamp and gravel beach, a mile and a half in length. Above it towered a tapering mountain whose flanks were scarred by an enormous shell-shaped gash. Here, a century or so before, a huge side of the mountain had fallen away, burying an Indian village. Now, beneath the scarred mountain, the city of Dawson began to grow.

Joe Ladue was the city's founder. While other men rushed up Bonanza to stake gold claims, Ladue staked out a square mile of swampy ground at the river's mouth and divided it into city lots. He knew that the boom he had been waiting for had come at last. Before two years had passed, some of these lots were worth twenty thousand dollars.

Ladue lost no time in building a log cabin, opening a saloon, and moving his sawmill to the site of the new stampede. Thus, he was able to supply the three things that men seem to want most in a gold camp: whisky, dressed lumber, and land. All around his cabin, little tents began to spring up. Within two years the entire flat and the hills around would be white with them.

Still, no one knew how much gold there was in the Klondike. A group of early prospectors, meeting together two days after Carmack's strike, had optimistically changed the name of Rabbit Creek to Bonanza. But most old-timers were skeptical of any real riches under the eighteen-inch carpet of spongy wet moss that covered the entire valley.

Indeed, it was more often than not the newcomers—"cheechakos," as the Indians called them—who got the richest ground. The old-timers, or "sourdoughs," simply wouldn't believe in it. Two of them came down from Indian River a few days after the strike and stopped at the Klondike, where they heard the news.

"Shall we go up and stake?" one of them asked the other.

"I wouldn't go across the river on that old Siwash's word," was the reply.

They kept right on going to Fortymile, where, to their astonishment, they found the town deserted.

Louis Rhodes, a Fortymile prospector, was trudging up Bonanza, above Carmack's discovery, wondering whether or not he should bother to stake. He met a man on claim *Twenty* who had given up in disgust.

"I'll leave it to the Swedes," the man cried. The Swedes were supposed to be notorious for staking poor ground.

Rhodes trudged on five hundred feet to claim *Twenty-one.*

Here, on the newly cut stakes, was a derisive sign: "This moose pasture is reserved for Swedes and cheechakos."

On an impulse Rhodes cut his own name into the stakes which had been abandoned by the previous claimant. Then he wondered why he'd bothered. He turned to a companion and remarked that for two bits he'd cut his name off again.

Fortunately, he didn't. Before spring the claim had produced forty thousand dollars.

By early September, Bonanza had been staked for thirteen miles and there were five hundred men in the Klondike Valley looking for new fields to conquer. The new fields weren't long in coming.

One memorable morning a black-bearded man named William Johns came hiking down Bonanza Valley, disgusted because there was no ground left to stake. He was a former newspaperman who had drifted north looking for gold. So far he had found none. When he and his partner came back to the collection of shacks that had sprung up near Carmack's claim, they found that several men were missing and no one seemed to know where they were. A strange, indefinable feeling was in the air. The day before, several men had been exploring a fork of Bonanza Creek. This was the same fork that Carmack and the Indians had passed just before they made their discovery. Johns and his partner, Fred Bruceth, decided to go up and have a look. On the way they met another miner, who tried to put them off. The two men grew suspicious and began to hurry along through the undergrowth.

Suddenly Bruceth stopped short and pointed down at the creek.

"Somebody's working," he said. "The water's muddy."

An electric feeling ran through them. They pressed on, like hunters scenting game, alert and silent. They turned a corner in the valley and came suddenly upon four excited men. Three of them were crowded around the other, who held a pan in his hand. They looked up, as Johns later reported, "like cats caught with a cream pitcher." For there was at least fifty cents' worth of gold in that pan. Other men began to arrive momentarily, as if some seventh sense had called them, and soon everybody was furiously staking claims. The new creek was quickly named Eldorado. None realized it then, but it was far richer than Bonanza. The forty good claims on this creek were each to produce a million dollars or more. But not for William Johns. He sold his share for just eight hundred dollars.

The man holding the pan that day was Antone Stander, a romantic-looking Austrian with thick, wavy hair and a poet's face. He staked *Six* Eldorado and went off to Fortymile to record it. But he had no money to work the claim. He tried to borrow from the Alaska Commercial Company, but found he had to have somebody to guarantee his loan. He asked the help of a chance acquaintance, a burly young man named Clarence Berry. Berry agreed, and Stander gratefully made him his partner.

For Berry, a penniless fruit farmer from Fresno, California, this was the start of a great fortune. He had brought his young bride into the Yukon over the Chilkoot Pass the previous year. All winter he had worked at odd jobs to make ends meet. Now, though he did not yet know it, he was on the verge of becoming a millionaire.

And yet all this time nobody was sure whether or not there was gold in any quantity on the Klondike. To discover the worth of a placer claim, it is necessary to sink a shaft to bedrock. This nobody had yet been able to do, for the bedrock was twenty feet below the mossy surface of the ground.

Nowhere in the world is placer-mining a more difficult job than it is in the Yukon. The ground is frozen hard as granite two feet below the surface, and before the earth can be dug it must be thawed. In those days the only method was to thaw it with wood fires. The miners would build a fire and the ground would thaw for two feet. The soft earth would be shoveled away and a new fire built. Slowly, two feet at a time, the men would burn their way deep into the earth until they reached the hard shale in which the gold was to be found.

It might take several shafts, each dug laboriously in this manner, to find what was known as the "paystreak." These paystreaks, several feet wide and full of gold dust and nuggets, were really the bottoms of ancient stream beds. But they bore no relation to the present stream, for they meandered backward and forward across the valley in an unpredictable serpent's course. The only way to find them was to dig for them.

Once at the bottom of a shaft, the miners dug tunnels, or "drifts" as they called them, along the bedrock. If gold was found, the paydirt was hoisted up in buckets and piled in a dump. Later, in the spring when the water ran again, this dump would be sluiced out for its gold.

The early days of the Klondike strike were restless ones. Many miners were so excited that they couldn't settle down to dig shafts. Others were too skeptical to bother. Many more simply didn't have the funds to purchase equipment. As a result, claims began to change hands and many men lost and won fortunes without knowing it.

The classic example involved a prospector named Charley Anderson, who, for the rest of his life, was known as the Lucky Swede. Anderson bought claim *Twenty-nine* on Eldorado when he was drunk. He paid every cent he had for it—eight hundred dollars. The following day he tried without success to get his money back. Disconsolate at his loss, he went out to work the supposedly worthless ground. In just four years he took one million two hundred thousand dollars from it.

Next to *Twenty-nine* was Number *Thirty,* staked by Russian John Zarnowsky. Food was short in Dawson that winter, and Russian John traded his claim away for a sack of flour. The man who got it was a big, lumbering Nova Scotian, "Big Alec" McDonald. This claim was the cornerstone for the most enormous fortune in the Yukon. Before Big Alec was through, he was worth an estimated twenty million and had become the most famous man in the north. They called him the King of the Klondike.

Another famous transaction involved Professor Thomas Lippy, a muscular young man from Seattle, Washington, who had been physical education instructor and secretary of the Seattle Y.M.C.A. One day early in 1896 Lippy had a crazy hunch. Without hesitation he quit his job and, with his wife and adopted son, set off for the Yukon. The trio climbed the Chilkoot Pass and drifted down the river. They passed the mouth of the Klondike at the psychological moment: Eldorado was just being staked. Lippy rushed up the creek in time to stake *Thirty-six.* Then he tried to build a cabin, only to discover that the claim was high above the timber line. As a result, he traded it off for Number *Sixteen* farther down the valley, where the timber was heavy. It was one of history's luckiest trades. *Thirty-six* produced little gold; *Sixteen* yielded Lippy more than a million dollars.

All this time, while men bought and sold their claims, while

Joe Ladue's sawmill was busily turning out sluice-box lumber, while rough little cabins were springing up in Dawson City, Louis Rhodes was quietly burning his way down to bedrock. He was determined to find out whether there really were millions under the moose pasture. Finally he reached the bottom, and in the candlelight he caught the glitter of gold. It was all around him, in a paystreak four feet wide. He could pull the nuggets right out of the gravel. Rhodes, looking at them, must have thanked his Maker that he hadn't cut his name off those stakes. He hauled up a bucket of dirt on his windlass, filled a pan, swirled out the gravel, and weighed the gold that was left behind. In that one pan there was more than sixty-five dollars in dust and nuggets. The news ran like an electric shock up and down the creek. There was no doubt now that Bonanza was rich beyond men's wildest dreams.

But Eldorado was richer. A few days later Clarence Berry reached bedrock. His first pan yielded fifty-seven dollars. A later pan yielded eighty. Another yielded one hundred and twelve. On *Sixteen* Eldorado four coal-miners from Nanaimo, British Columbia, got two hundred twelve dollars from a single pan. This was considered almost unbelievable by the old prospectors who, until this time, had considered a twenty-five-cent pan a wonderful prospect. And yet before the winter was over, some men would be getting as high as eight hundred dollars from a single pan of paydirt.

Now Bonanza and Eldorado creeks became the scenes of wild activity. The whole valley was pungent with the smell of wood smoke and ringing with the sound of ax and hammer. At night the skies were scarlet with the fitful glow of hundreds of fires as men began to burn their way to the golden bedrock.

Wages rose to fifteen dollars a day and sometimes more. Clarence Berry began to hire as many men as he could lay his hands on. He paid them every night, simply taking a panful of dirt from the dump and washing out an ounce of gold in a washtub at the back of his cabin. When Mrs. Berry wanted pocket money, she walked out to the dump with a goldpan and helped herself to a few hundred dollars.

In the meantime, Bob Henderson had been working away at his Gold Bottom claim, just over the hills. Perhaps he wondered idly what had become of George Carmack. One day he found out.

Looking up, he saw two men coming down the narrow valley from the Dome above.

"Where are you boys from?" Henderson asked.

"Bonanza," was the reply.

Henderson had never heard of Bonanza. Being a proud man, he didn't like to show his ignorance of the country. Finally, however, he ventured to ask.

The men pointed back over the hill. "Rabbit Creek," they said.

"What have you got there?" Henderson asked, puzzled.

"We've got the biggest thing in the world!"

"Who found it?" Henderson asked, his heart sinking.

"Carmack."

Henderson threw down his shovel in a gesture of despair and then went over and sat down by the side of the creek, so sick at heart he could say no more. Carmack had not kept his promise.

Nor was this the end of Henderson's misfortunes.

In the interim he had found a spot on Gold Bottom where the pay ran to thirty-five cents a pan. This was big money to Henderson, and he decided to stake it as a discovery claim. Off he went down the creek, heading for Fortymile to record his find. On the way he met a middleaged German named Andrew Hunker. Hunker had come up from Bonanza by way of the Klondike and was only now entering Henderson's territory. But on the way up, on the other branch of Henderson's creek, he had found ground which yielded three dollars to the pan.

Henderson was in a dilemma. Obviously the other fork of the creek was much richer than the one he'd been working. Should he cling to his discovery claim on the poor ground, or relinquish it for an ordinary claim on the rich ground? By law he could stake only one claim in any one district. In the end, he gave up his discovery and staked next to Hunker. Thus

Hunker, not Henderson, was hailed as the discoverer of Gold Bottom Creek and the name was changed to Hunker Creek. It turned out to be one of the richest creeks in the Klondike.

Henderson still might have become a rich man, but Fate was not yet through with him. In those hard days on Indian River he had sustained a painful leg injury, and this now returned to plague him. All winter he was sick and unable to work his ground, as the law demanded. Finally he was forced to sell the claim to pay doctors' bills. He got three thousand dollars for it. In the end it produced hundreds of thousands.

A year later, sick, discouraged, and embittered, Henderson finally made his way out to the Alaska coastline and took a steamer for Seattle. For all of his years in the Yukon he had just eleven hundred dollars in gold dust tied up in a caribou-hide poke. By the time he reached Seattle that was gone, too. For Henderson this was the bitter end. He tore the badge of the Yukon Order of Pioneers from his lapel and handed it to a chance acquaintance. "You keep this," he said, "I'll lose it, too. I'm not fit to live among civilized men."

And yet, for the rest of his life, to the day of his death in 1933, he continued to search for gold. He searched in vain. In the end the Canadian government granted him a pension of two hundred dollars a month in recognition of that August day when he had persuaded George Carmack to take a memorable trip up the Klondike.

CHAPTER 3

THE RICHEST POOR MEN IN THE WORLD

SUCH WAS THE ISOLATION OF THE YUKON RIVER country that it took almost a year for the news of the great strike to reach the outside world. Even as late as Christmas 1896, four months after Carmack's discovery, the residents of Circle City, Alaska, had heard only faint whispers of the excitement on the Klondike.

In Circle, as at Fortymile, men first refused to believe their ears when stray travelers arrived in town to report that men were getting an ounce to the pan and better on the tributaries of the salmon stream. But the reports kept filtering in, and, in twos and threes, men began to leave by dog team over the winter ice to the new diggings.

Then, one day early in January, Arthur Treadwell Walden, a

young dog-puncher, arrived from Dawson with a load of mail. He walked into Harry Ash's saloon and ordered a cup of beef tea, for dog-drivers knew better than to drink whisky in the wintertime. Harry Ash didn't get around to filling the order. He picked a letter out of the pile, tore it open, read it swiftly, and leaped over the bar.

"Boy!" he shouted. "Help yourself to the whole shooting-match! I'm off to the Klondike!"

The letter confirmed what had for some time been rumored. The new diggings were the richest in history. A wild orgy followed. Men knocked the necks off bottles in Ash's saloon and the entire town went on a spree. Harry Ash left town the next morning and the whole population of four hundred souls followed behind him, strung out in a long, straggling line down the frozen Yukon.

Dogs, which had once sold for twenty-five dollars apiece in Circle, now commanded prices as high as fifteen hundred dollars. Cabins worth five hundred dollars the previous day were now valueless. The news from the Klondike turned Circle City into a ghost town. Those men who failed to get dogs loaded their sleds and tugged them by hand the four hundred cold, lonely miles to Dawson.

Sometimes the men toiling along the river looked curiously at a thin and delicate Jesuit priest moving slowly with a single husky dog. He had a rope over his shoulder and was helping the dog pull his heavy sled, which contained very little food but was crammed with medical supplies. This was Father William Judge, and he was interested in souls, not gold. He was determined to start a hospital in Dawson City, for he knew that frontier boomtowns breed typhoid, scurvy, malaria, and pneumonia. In the end he succeeded in saving hundreds of lives, but he himself was to die within two years of fatigue in the hospital that became his monument.

Meanwhile, confusion reigned on the Klondike. In the first wild rush to Bonanza, men had hammered in their stakes everywhere and anywhere. As a result, many claims were not properly located. Some were too big. Others were too small. Disputes arose and quarrels started. Men jumped one another's claims and fought for the rich ground.

In the end, the miners decided to ask William Ogilvie, the government surveyor, to make a proper survey of both Eldorado and Bonanza and allot each man his proper share. Ogilvie had been in the country for years. He was a tough, incorruptible man, with a grave face and a black spade beard which masked a propensity for practical jokes. He started his survey in January and finished it in May. During these months William Ogilvie had dozens of chances to become a wealthy man. But because he did not believe that a public servant should use his special knowledge for private gain, he refused to stake any ground and remained a comparatively poor man while all around him men came into millions.

This did not apply to his employees, notably an assistant named Dick Lowe. As soon as Ogilvie began to survey each claim, he found that many were longer than the five hundred feet the law allowed. This left slivers of ground, known as "fractions," between many properties. Lowe, a former mule-skinner from the Black Hills of Colorado, staked one of these tiny fractions. It was just sixty-five feet wide, hardly big enough to work, and Lowe, who was looking for something larger, staked it rather reluctantly. But the thin wedge of moss-covered earth became famous as the Dick Lowe Fraction. It yielded six hundred thousand dollars in gold dust and was, perhaps, the richest single parcel of land on the globe.

By now there were close to fifteen hundred people, almost all of them men, living in Dawson City. And here, in this town of newly minted millionaires, money would buy very little. Food was so scarce that men had to kill their dogs because they could no longer feed them. Prices soared. A box of laundry starch cost two hundred fifty dollars and laundry service became so expensive that most men wore their shirts until they could stand them no longer, then threw them away. One enterprising French-Canadian salvaged these discarded shirts, washed and pressed them, and then sold them back to the original owners as new garments.

"Swiftwater" Bill Gates had the only white shirt in town. He was so proud of it that while it was being laundered he went to bed. Swiftwater was rapidly becoming Dawson's leading character. Later on, in order to spite a lady friend who was cold to him, he bought up every egg in town for a dollar apiece. The lady liked eggs and Swiftwater was determined that she wouldn't get any. He could afford to do these things because he owned a piece of one of the richest claims on Eldorado, Number *Thirteen*. He made so much money that the following year, in Seattle, he took a bath in champagne. Soon after this, Swiftwater Bill Gates was dead broke.

But there were few men as prosperous as Swiftwater Bill that first winter. An ironic situation was developing in Dawson. Here was a town full of men who owned claims worth millions of dollars. Yet many of them were too broke to buy the necessary equipment to work the ground. Some borrowed money from professional lenders at the exorbitant interest rate of ten percent per month. Others let their claims out on a lease, or a "lay" as it was called.

Under this "lay" arrangement, the laymen would undertake to work the owner's claim for a season and then pay him a certain percentage—usually half—of what they found. Many men who had not struck it rich in the beginning became wealthy in this way. Others worked hard all winter on a lay only to find the claim was worthless.

Others sold their claims outright for what seemed a good sum at the time but later proved to be a pittance. Often a claim-owner would accept a small down payment and take the rest at a later date. Several enterprising men bought claims in this way. They would pay a small amount down and then go out to the claim, dig out a quantity of paydirt, and pay the owner for the claim with his own gold.

The shrewdest and most enterprising man of all was Big Alec McDonald, the ponderous, black-haired Nova Scotian who had traded a sack of flour for a rich Eldorado claim. McDonald, who had only three dollars to his name, let the claim out on a lay. But he didn't stop there. He began to borrow money at the exorbitant rates and buy interests in other men's claims. He would make the smallest possible down payment and promise to pay off the balance by the following July. Soon he owned interests in forty claims in the Klondike district. By July he would either be the richest man in the world, or the biggest bankrupt.

McDonald chose the month of July to promise final payments because the spring clean-ups were made in May and June. It was impossible to sink shafts and dig out paydirt during the summer because after the spring thaw the creek valleys turned into giant swamps. All the actual mining was done in the winter. Men hauled the dirt from the tunnels day after day and piled it in huge dumps. In the spring they built sluice boxes to wash out the gold. These were long, slender, open boxes with cross bars, or "riffles," nailed at intervals along the bottom. When the snow melted and the ice was out of the creeks, the miners diverted water from the stream and sent it coursing down these boxes. Men at the upper end shoveled gravel in from the dump. The water washed the gravel down through the box, but the heavier gold was left behind, caught in the riffles. Every few days the box was taken up and the gold panned out of the bottom. It was not until this spring clean-up that a claim-owner knew the exact richness of his property or the results of his winter's labor.

In the spring of 1897 the thaw came late. It was almost too late for Big Alec. He was still taking gold from his sluice boxes when the deadline for the payment of his debts arrived. If he didn't have enough, his property would revert to the original owners. He weighed out his gold anxiously. There was just enough to pay his debts. Now he owned more property than any single man on the Klondike.

Soon Big Alec's packtrains of fifteen or twenty mules became a familiar sight moving down the Klondike Valley to the Bank of British North America in Dawson. Each of these mules carried twenty thousand dollars' worth of nuggets in sacks on its back. McDonald's stature became so great that it was said that if he stopped by a man's claim for a moment and looked at it, the property instantly doubled in value. At the peak of his success he was said to be worth twenty million dollars. He toured Europe, ate off gold plate, and married a London society girl. Yet in the end he, like so many other Klondike Kings, died penniless in a little log cabin, alone in the wilderness.

For the entire winter Dawson had lived in almost complete isolation, cut off from the outside world. In January, William Ogilvie had managed to get news of the strike out to the government in Ottawa by a dog-puncher who carried the mail to Juneau on the Pacific Coast. But his news was meager, and when it was published in the form of an official government paper it caused little excitement. Newly washed gold was being taken out by the ton. Clarence Berry alone had washed out one hundred thirty thousand dollars in his spring clean-up. But of this the outside world knew nothing at all.

Nor did Dawson know what was going on in the outside world. It might, indeed, have been a town on another planet. The last arrivals in January had brought the latest news: Queen Victoria lay critically ill, Pope Leo XIII was on the point of death, war seemed imminent between England and Russia, and an exciting heavyweight fight was planned between James J. Corbett and Bob Fitzsimmons. Until late in May no further scrap of news reached the town.

By May there was hardly any food left in Dawson. Joe Ladue's saloon was reduced to selling water lightly flavored with whisky for fifty cents a glass. All the flour and bacon was gone, and the camp was subsisting on beans. Then on May 14 the ice in the Yukon broke with a great roar and went rushing off sixteen hundred miles to the Bering Sea.

Across the Klondike, on the flat where Carmack had once dried salmon, was the neighboring town of Klondike City, or, as everybody called it, "Lousetown." The saloonkeepers in Lousetown knew that as soon as the ice broke, boats would be pouring down the river to the new diggings. They put up a sign which read: "Danger Below: Keep to the Right." Early on May 16 the first boatloads of men arrived, saw the sign, and landed at Lousetown, thinking it was Dawson. The saloons began to do a roaring business.

Joe Ladue, over in Dawson, swore mightily. He and William Ogilvie rushed to the Ladue sawmill and tied the steamwhistle open. The new arrivals heard it and rushed across the Klondike. "What's the news?" asked one of the Dawson men. Back came the reply: "The Pope's alive, the Queen's well, there's no war, and Bob Fitzsimmons knocked hell out of Jim Corbett."

Before long a wilderness of tents had sprung up. Boats of all kinds—rafts, scows, launches, bayeux, and Peterborough canoes—began to arrive at all hours. Starving men rushed to the newcomers' boats and offered fantastic prices for food. Bacon purchased at eleven cents a pound now sold for seventy-five cents. Tea worth twenty-five cents sold for two dollars.

There were only two children in Dawson at this time, a sixteen-year-old boy named Monte Snow and his fourteen-year-old sister. Monte Snow's father, George Snow, was an old-time theatrical man who had once co-starred with the famous actor Edwin Booth in California. The Snow family had drifted north, playing in theaters from Seattle to Juneau. Finally, when Monte was twelve and his sister ten, they climbed the Chilkoot and drifted down the river, costumes and all, to Circle City.

Here George Snow opened an opera house and began producing plays such as *Uncle Tom's Cabin* and *Rip Van Winkle*. Monte and his sister were onstage every night. There was plenty of money for an energetic boy to make in those days. One evening young Monte picked up one hundred forty-two dollars in nuggets flung onto the stage by applauding prospectors.

But there was more money in Dawson now than in Circle City. The Snow family hadn't come down in the first rush because they simply couldn't believe that George Carmack had found gold. Young Monte sold his three husky dogs for five hundred dollars to a stampeding prospector and considered he'd made a tidy profit. Finally, as the town emptied, the Snows went along, too. They landed in Dawson on May 23.

The first man that Monte recognized when he walked down Front Street was Harry Ash, the former Circle City saloon-keeper. Ash had opened a saloon in Dawson. It consisted only of a tent with a floor for dancing and a gambling-table and bar at the rear. In front of the gold scales was a space six feet long and three feet wide covered with sawdust.

"Here, Monte," said Harry Ash, "take two sacks and go down to Joe Ladue's sawmill for me and get some fresh saw-dust. I'll give you the old stuff and you can pan it out and keep what you get."

This didn't seem like very good pay to Monte Snow, and he said so.

Ash shrugged. "Okay, I'll give you twenty-five dollars, sight unseen, for whatever you get from that sawdust."

The boy was shrewd enough to realize that the sawdust must have more gold in it than he'd figured. He said he'd agree to the original deal. He was glad he did. He panned the saw-dust for two hours and a quarter and took out two hundred seventy-eight dollars worth of gold, which had filtered down from miners' pokes as they walked up to the gold scales. This was more money than many full-grown men were making on the creeks.

The following month the first steamboat arrived in Dawson—the Alaska Commercial Company's sternwheeler *Bella*. She was loaded to the gunwales with liquor and food.

The saloons threw their doors open and served free drinks to everybody. By sundown the whole town was drunk.

And still the world did not know about the Klondike. For these first arrivals were mainly men who had come into the Yukon district attracted by earlier reports of gold at Fortymile or Circle City. Many of them were surprised to find a new town at the mouth of a river they had never heard of.

Dawson now boasted a population of twenty-five hundred souls. Every square inch in the Klondike had been staked. And yet the great Gold Rush had hardly begun.

CHAPTER 4

THE GREAT RUSH BEGINS

DAWSON WAS FULL OF MEN WHO HAD MADE FORtunes overnight. Many of them had been five or ten years or more in the country. All had led hard lives. For an entire winter they had been doing heavy physical work on their claims, living in tiny, uncomfortable cabins and subsisting on beans and hardtack. Their days had been spent at the bottom of mine-shafts, where the acrid smoke of wood fires burned their eyes and throats. Their nights had been spent in unlit cabins so cold that the steam escaping from the green logs turned to ice when the fire went out, and formed a glacier on the dirt floor.

Now the big sternwheel steamer *Portus B. Weare* was tied up at the riverbank, ready to leave for civilization. It had followed the little *Bella* into Dawson. In a few hours every available berth was booked.

The big white steamer puffed out into the center of the river with its cargo of miners aboard, its scarlet paddlewheel churning up the yellow waters, its twin black stacks belching white wood-smoke. In the purser's cabin lay a ton and a half of gold. On the decks was more gold tied up in blankets or boxes or moosehide pokes. There was so much gold that the decks had to be shored up with timbers to prevent them from caving in before the steamer could leave.

For eight days the *Weare* slid down the broad, swift Yukon, following the twists and turns of the river up and back across the Arctic Circle until it reached the hundreds of channels at the delta. Finally the steamer came out onto the cold Bering Sea and the little town of St. Michael. Here the eighty-odd miners went on a food spree. They bought apple cider, canned pineapple, dried apricots, bottled cherries—all the luxuries they had gone so long without. They stuffed themselves full. Then they embarked on two small, grubby ocean vessels, the *Excelsior* destined for San Francisco, and the *Portland* for Seattle. It was a long, weary trip, more than three thousand miles. Many of the men were seasick. Those who weren't drank champagne for most of the voyage.

It is pleasant to imagine the feelings of these men as they waited impatiently for the ships to dock at the two Pacific Coast cities. Most of them had gone to the Yukon as a last resort. The entire continent in those days was plunged into one of the worst depressions in history. It was so bad that the people of the Pacific northwest, unable to buy food, were living on clams dug up on the beaches. As one Congressman remarked, they had eaten so many clams their stomachs rose and fell with the tides.

Now here were Clarence Berry, the Fresno fruit farmer, and Tom Lippy, the Y.M.C.A. man, and Louis Rhodes, the Fortymile prospector, and Joe Ladue, the French-Canadian trader, and eighty or more others, about to arrive among their families with sacks of gold.

The *Excelsior* landed first in San Francisco, on July 17, 1897. The news of her coming preceded her, and there was a crowd on the dock to meet her when she arrived. Surely no more dramatic scene ever greeted watchers on any dock! In single file down the gangway came fifteen men from the Klondike, dressed just as they had been when they left their claims. Their grizzled, unshaven faces were shaded by broad-brimmed miner's hats; their worn and tattered clothing hung on their gaunt figures in shreds; their high boots were still flecked with the clay of Bonanza and Eldorado creeks.

As each man came down the gangway, he struggled with his load of gold. Some who had blankets with fifty thousand dollars strapped in them had to call for help from the dock. The crowd parted in awe to let the men go past. Then, as the excitement mounted, the whole throng began to follow the men up the street.

The Klondikers marched straight to Selby's smelting-works on Montgomery Street. Here, with scores crowding behind them, they proceeded to lay half a million dollars' worth of gold dust on the counter. Buckskin bags and dirty canvas containers were ripped open. Glass fruit jars and jelly tumblers covered with writing paper and secured by twine were produced from pockets. The bags and boxes and jars were torn apart, the contents weighed out, and the miners paid in new bills for their gold.

No spectacle comparable to this had taken place in San Francisco since the days of 1849.

This was only the beginning. There were sixty-eight more Klondikers aboard the *Portland,* due in Seattle in two days. The entire Pacific Coast was aflame with excitement. The Seattle papers dispatched boatloads of reporters to board the *Portland* the moment she steamed into Puget Sound. When the news flashed across the city that she had arrived, thousands streamed down to Schwabacher's wharf to greet her.

One of the newspapermen estimated the weight of gold aboard the treasure ship. It came to more than a ton. That phrase "a ton of gold" flashing across the news wires to every city, town, and hamlet on the continent, and thence to Europe,

New Zealand, South Africa, and Australia, fired the imagination of the world.

The Klondikers were heroes. Their stories, often exaggerated and badly garbled, were told and retold until they became legends. Tom Lippy and his wife, occupying an expensive suite in a San Francisco hotel, had to blockade themselves from reporters who jammed the corridors outside. Clarence Berry's one hundred thirty thousand dollars in nuggets went on display in a jeweler's window, and crowds milled around it.

Joe Ladue was mobbed. Everywhere the swarthy little French-Canadian went, crowds followed him. All he wanted to do was go back to Schuyler Falls, New York, where his sweetheart was waiting for him. He had tried to marry her years before, but her family had refused to allow the match because Ladue was too poor. Now they welcomed him with open arms.

Poor Joe Ladue! So many people crowded into the family farmhouse that he finally threw his nuggets onto the table for all to see and went out to hide in the barn. Fortune, romance, and security were his. He was rich and famous. His name became a byword and the President himself sent to see him. But the long, hard Yukon years had taken their toll. All Joe Ladue wanted was rest.

Lincoln Steffens, the greatest reporter of his day, interviewed him at this time. "He is the weariest-looking man I ever saw," he wrote. Ladue had not long to enjoy his fortune. Tuberculosis was already ravaging his lungs. In a little more than a year, at the peak of the great Gold Rush, Joe Ladue would be dead.

Other stories had happier endings. Perhaps the most dramatic was the Cinderella tale of "Papa" William Stanley, a lame old bookseller from Seattle. In the spring of '96, Stanley and his family were destitute, with nowhere to turn. As a last resort the old man and his son decided to go to the Yukon to seek their fortune. To make ends meet, Mrs. Stanley took in washing. Her husband and son might have been swallowed up by the earth, for all she knew. No word of them seeped out of the Yukon. Then, more than a year later, she received an unbelievable message: her husband had just arrived on the *Portland* with a hundred thousand dollars in gold dust. Mrs. Stanley was scrubbing her customer's washing when she heard the news. She dropped her scrubbing brush and never picked it up again. She threw away her own threadbare dresses, moved into a handsome hotel suite, and spent the following week on a shopping spree while newspapermen crowded at her elbow.

The news from the Klondike ended the great depression of the nineties within seven days. In every town on the continent, men left their jobs and made plans to head north. Clerks leaped counters and rushed to the shipping offices to buy tickets. Doctors left their patients. Ministers quit their churches. The *Seattle Times* lost most of its reporters. The Seattle police force lost half its policemen. Hordes of firemen joined the ranks of the gold-seekers, to the consternation of municipal authorities. A few days after the gold ships landed, the mayor of Seattle, who was in San Francisco attending a convention, wired his resignation and joined the ranks of men pushing north.

In the coastal towns, grocers doubled their staffs, outfitting stores ran day and night, and clothing shops sold out of blankets and woolens. In San Francisco, the day after the *Excelsior* arrived, the Alaska Commercial Company's offices were besieged by men. The ship's berths were sold out in a matter of hours, and ten times the number of purchasers had to be turned away. Within forty-eight hours of the *Portland*'s arrival in Seattle, hundreds of men were equipped and ready to go north.

By August, towns as far away as Winnipeg were cleaned out of furs and sleeping-robes. Seattle, San Francisco, Victoria, and Vancouver were jammed with gold-seekers. The streets around the docks were alive with men. Traffic at the waterfront was hopelessly snarled. The sidewalks were piled high with provisions. Every conceivable beast of burden—horses, oxen, goats, mules, and dogs of all descriptions—made their way slowly through the gesticulating crowds, loaded with supplies for the Klondike. By autumn it was estimated that ten thousand men had passed through Seattle alone. By spring the number had reached sixty thousand.

Ships of every description were pressed into service to take the stampeders north. They were brought in from all over the globe, from China, South Africa, India, and Australia. Many were leaky, ancient tubs resurrected from the boneyards and patched up to make a single trip. Not a few foundered en route. Others were former cattle boats or coal boats hastily refurbished to hold five or ten times the normal number of passengers.

The tiny steamship *Amur,* with space for sixty aboard, managed to cram in five hundred, not to mention five hundred dogs, by squeezing ten men into each cabin.

The steamer *Bristol* sailed out of Victoria with six hundred horses tethered on her decks. The cargo was so heavy that after being out a day the vessel had to return to port to readjust her top load.

On the steamer *Islander* the horses were wedged together so tightly that they couldn't lie down. Their heads were all up against the engines. When the ship got under way, the throbbing of the motors drove the animals berserk and they began to thrash and kick and throw themselves against their halters in a welter of heaving flesh.

In Seattle the old coal-carrier *Williamette* was pressed into service. The owners jammed eight hundred passengers and three hundred animals aboard her. Coal dust still hung heavily in the air, so that everything—cargo, men, and horses—was soon grimy with it. As for the decks, they were so jammed with hay and freight that it was impossible to look out on the ocean.

Men, women, and children rushed north, jammed together like cattle in the holds of the creaking old ships. Bert Parker, a seventeen-year-old boy from Guelph, Ontario, was one of them. He had scraped together two hundred dollars, crossed the continent, and now found himself jammed aboard an old Chinese freighter called the *Ning Chow.* She was one of the largest boats ever to go up the Pacific Coast. Parker later described this and other experiences of the stampede. He recalled that there were almost a thousand passengers on the boat, together with uncounted horses, dogs, and jackasses. He slept in a rough lumber bunk belowdecks. The bunks were four-deckers, and the ship rolled so badly that Parker was sick, along with almost everybody else. The food was so bad that an irate Texan tried to shoot the dining-room steward, but was prevented. Finally Parker found himself dumped unceremoniously on the beach at Skagway along with thousands of others.

All that fall and winter the rush continued unabated. In Vancouver men tried to bribe ship's officers to let them aboard. Others went out into the streets and slugged ticket-holders, stole their fares, and took their places aboard ship.

All over the country men were forming themselves into associations for the purpose of exploiting Klondike gold. In Tacoma, Washington, the streetcar employees held a mass meeting and nominated nine men to be outfitted for the Klondike. These men were to stake claims and prospect for the others.

In Chicago a group of spiritualists held a meeting and gazed into the infinite. As a result, they drew up some maps which they said they had obtained with the assistance of the spirit world, and sent one of their number north to seek fortunes for all of them.

In the same city a group of gamblers, uprooted from their places of business by a reform movement, held a mass meeting in a downtown saloon and decided to leave for the Klondike en masse. They departed three hours later, taking as luggage nothing more than some heavy underwear and a set of gold scales.

By winter there were one hundred and fifty co-operative syndicates bearing the name Klondike. There were barbers' syndicates to shave bewhiskered miners. There were settlement companies to establish farms. And one curious group announced it would establish a second city of Brooklyn in the far north.

The schemes grew stranger and stranger. One man announced he would establish a balloon route to the Klondike, and reservations poured in from all over the country. Another group proposed to set up "reindeer posts" all the way to Dawson City. A Milwaukee man decided to establish a carrier-pigeon service between the Klondike and Victoria, B.C. A New York syndicate declared it would build a bicycle path to the Yukon, and it promptly began to promote a special bicycle with a sidecar to carry one's outfit in.

A Pittsburgh man planned to establish a matrimonial agency on the Klondike and had no trouble at all recruiting single young women for it. A St. Louis bacteriologist announced he would leave at once with a pack full of deadly germs to kill Yukon mosquitoes. A Seattle man claimed he had perfected a way of condensing food so that a year's supply could be fitted into an ordinary valise.

The Chicago office of the North American Trading and Transportation Company, which ran steamers on the Yukon River, was besieged by crackpots. A lady crystal-gazer cornered the president, Portus B. Weare, in his office. She said she could find nuggets by staring into a crystal ball and wanted him to give her two thousand dollars to go to the Klondike.

A man who wrote cheap detective stories had an equally ingenious suggestion. He wanted Weare to give him several thousand dollars so that he could go to the Yukon, arrest any notorious criminals that might have drifted there, and collect the reward money.

In short, the whole world was Klondike-crazy. The magic name was on everybody's lips. It was impossible to open a newspaper without seeing the word applied to everything from spectacles to false teeth. For almost six months it occupied the front pages to the virtual exclusion of other news.

And in all this time only the merest handful of men had actually reached Dawson City.

CHAPTER 5

THREE THOUSAND DYING HORSES

THE UPPER YUKON COUNTRY IS WALLED OFF from the Pacific coastline by a range of high sawtooth mountains. In this wall, nature has cut two narrow notches. One of these notches is the Chilkoot Pass, the other the White Pass. It was through these two passes that the bulk of the gold-seekers made their way in the autumn, winter, and spring of 1897–98.

The gateway to the Chilkoot was the sprawling, brawling beach town of Dyea, at the end of a long narrow arm of the sea. The gateway to the White Pass was the rival town of Skagway, at the end of a twin fjord. Of the two mountain passes, the Chilkoot is probably the more notorious in song, story, and legend. But in those early days of the Gold Rush, in the fall of 1897, the White Pass was a hell on earth.

The only occupant of the Skagway beach in the days before the rush was an old steamboat captain and mail carrier named Billy Moore. He was in his mid-seventies and he sported a flowing white beard, but he thought nothing of mushing eight hundred miles alone through the white wilderness of the Yukon to bring the mail out from the diggings. When gold was struck on the Klondike, Billy Moore lost no time in staking out a town site at the head of the Skagway inlet, as Joe Ladue had done at Dawson City.

But when the men began to pour off the boats by the thousands and wade through the shallow tidewaters to the wooded delta of the Skagway River, no one paid any attention to Billy Moore's claims. There was no law in Skagway. Men made their own. They laid out a new town site with so little regard for Moore's rights that one of the streets went right through the center of his cabin. When Moore protested, they made him move his cabin. Only after years of litigation did the old man get the compensation due him.

The scenes on the Skagway beach in those first days of the rush are virtually indescribable. The water was so shallow that the ocean vessels had to anchor about a mile out at low tide. Passengers, dogs, horses, goats, and merchandise were ferried to shore in scows at twenty-five cents a load. The beach itself was a confused welter of packing-cases, duffel bags, packsacks, boxes, shouting men, and terrified animals. The scows dumped their cargoes at the sea's edge and headed back to the ships for another payload. As the tide began to rise, men frantically tried to move their goods to a higher spot. The sea was full of floating boxes, soaking sacks of flour, and drowning animals. Men in rubber boots floundered about. Boats of all shapes and sizes dotted the inlet, coming and going. The air was full of sound and fury: horses neighing, men cursing and shouting, whistles blowing, axes felling trees.

In the woods beyond, the city of Skagway was taking shape. Tents of every description went up. Groups of men stood around sheet-iron stoves cooking meals. Hay was piled everywhere. Streets were slowly being hacked through the forest. To a newcomer the spectacle was one of utter confusion, and this was enhanced by the fact that the town changed daily. Tents moved; new cabins appeared; restaurants were established, then shifted. Nothing was stable.

Moving ceaselessly through this confusion was a liquid line of men and animals heading up the river valley toward the pass that led through the mountains. For men were frantic to get over the trail before the snows fell and the river froze and all movement toward the Klondike ceased.

Each of these men had at least a ton of goods to hoist over the mountains. The Northwest Mounted Police who manned the border between Alaska and the Yukon would let nobody across unless he had a year's supply of food. In addition, men needed other equipment: saws, tools, pitch, and oakum to make boats to take them down the river; candles, matches, blankets, and furs; quicksilver, gold-pans, shovels, and picks for mining. Indeed, every conceivable item of merchandise from plate-glass windows to pianos was carried over the mountains on men's backs and floated down the river to Dawson.

All this paraphernalia had to be lugged in stages over the divide. To get a ton of goods across, a man might have to make twenty or more trips. Usually men moved their goods six miles at a time, cached them, and went back for another load. To move a ton of goods six miles, a man would have to trudge one hundred and twenty. Thus, although the distance from Skagway to the head of Yukon navigation at Lake Bennett was forty-five miles, many men walked a total of nine hundred miles to get there.

This backtracking, as it was called, was hard on men's nerves as well as on their physique. After the fifteenth trip or so, huge brawny men would fall down on the ground, bury their faces in their hands, and sob like children.

Hundreds of men had purchased horses and brought them north at great expense to do their packing for them. These wretched animals were almost useless. After the first few score of men and animals had struggled up the valley, through the mudholes and black swamps, over the boulder-strewn canyons, and onto the narrow trail that led around Porcupine Hill on the way to the summit, the Skagway Trail became a black mire. The horses, goaded, starved, beaten, and sworn at by inexperienced men, died by the hundreds. They floundered and drowned in the bottomless mudholes that marred the route. They slipped in the bogs and broke their legs. They lost their footing on the narrow mountain trails and plunged hundreds of feet to their death. But before they died, many of these unfortunate animals suffered the tortures of the damned.

One horse was seen to walk to the edge of the precipice on Porcupine Hill, gaze at the boulders below for a moment, then jump head-first onto them. The men who watched this incident were certain that the animal had committed suicide.

Those horses that survived the climb to the summit arrived at the Canadian border gaunt and spavined, their backs raw with terrible sores. It was the practice to unload the pack animals a quarter of a mile from the Mounted Police post and cover their backs with blankets in order to conceal these sores. For the redcoats would shoot sore horses on sight if they crossed the boundary.

By September there were three thousand dead horses lying along the trail between Skagway and the summit. Giant blowflies settled on their distended carcasses. The stench, blowing with the mountain winds onto the town of Skagway, was almost unbearable. It was said that men could walk the entire distance on the carcasses of pack animals.

Finally the trail became completely impassable, and by common consent it was closed while men toiled to build a corduroy road over the mud and the slime. As a route to the Klondike, it had been a complete fiasco, and the men who tried to breast it cursed the day they had been told that the White Pass was easier than the Chilkoot. The trail was littered with piles of goods and provisions which men had been forced to abandon because they could carry them no farther. Of the five thousand men who tried to cross the mountains that autumn by the Skagway Trail, scarcely five hundred reached the shores of Lake Bennett. The remainder turned back to Skagway. The hardiest waited there for the snows to fall and the trail to become passable again. Hundreds of others went back to their homes, thoroughly embittered, and never again spoke of the Klondike without a feeling of heartbreak and contempt.

CHAPTER 6

STARVATION! FLEE FOR YOUR LIVES!

DAWSON CITY, IN THAT FALL OF 1897, WAS FACING starvation.

During the summer the town had swelled until there were now almost five thousand people living in the Klondike area in tents or hastily constructed cabins. There were ten saloons, three restaurants, half a dozen hotels, and a theatrical company. Men were arriving daily by boat, scow, and raft. But there was not enough food in Dawson to last the winter.

True, every man who arrived brought a ton of supplies. But the fifteen men who had wintered the previous year were completely out of provisions. Several steamers were supposed to be on their way up from St. Michael, but winter was coming on fast and they had not yet arrived. It was a long, slow trip upriver, sixteen hundred miles against a stiff current, and often enough, as the water dropped in the fall, the heavily loaded vessels could not get across the shallow Yukon flats.

There were six steamboats desperately trying to reach Dawson before the river froze. Three of them, the *Portus B. Weare,* the *Charles Hamilton,* and the *John J. Healy,* belonged to the North American Trading and Transportation Company. The others, the *Bella, Alice,* and *Margaret,* belonged to the rival Alaska Commercial Company. The N.A.T. Company named its vessels after the company's directors. The A.C. Company was more gallant: it named its vessels after the directors' wives and daughters.

In Joe Ladue's old cabin the two companies were busy taking orders for winter supplies from hundreds of miners. These orders ran from one thousand to ten thousand dollars. Because of the desperate situation the companies refused to deliver a man more than two weeks' supply at any one time. This was to prevent, as far as possible, the evils of hoarding. Each man's goods, as they arrived, were piled in allotted stacks in the warehouses, but no man could take his entire share at once.

The *Margaret* finally reached Dawson, and Capt. J. E. Hansen, the manager of the A.C. Company, boarded her. He knew there were supplies at Fort Yukon at the head of the flats, and he hoped to be able to get some up to Dawson before freeze-up. But the river was dropping rapidly. When Hansen reached Fort Yukon he was greeted with the news that most of the other steamers were hopelessly aground on sandbars.

Hansen now knew that the situation was critical and that he must get back at top speed to warn the town. He started out in a birchbark canoe with a group of Indians, paddling with frenzied haste against the stiff current. Then the Indians deserted in a body and left him marooned on a sandbar without ax or bedding. Hansen was stranded here for five days, unable even to make a fire in the chill nights. Fortunately a chance boat came by and rescued him. At Circle City he got a second canoe and more Indians. Then, traveling day and night without sleep, he made one of the most rigorous trips on record back to Dawson, three hundred and fifty miles downriver from Fort Yukon.

Panic was already beginning to sweep Dawson before Hansen returned. The longed-for steamers had not arrived. Men were gathering in the streets in muttering throngs. Only one man refused to be panicked. This was Captain John J. Healy of the N.A.T. Company. He was a tough little man with cold, unflinching blue eyes and a small goatee, and he had spent most of his life on the frontier. He had been a sheriff in Missouri and an Indian scout. He was a member of two Blackfoot Indian tribes, and an old Yukon pioneer.

But he was not popular, because he was stiff and uncompromising, and now he was less popular than ever, for he stubbornly insisted that there would be enough provisions to last the winter. As if to prove his point, a steamboat whistle sounded out of the darkness late one evening. The whole town rushed to the riverbank. Healy could hardly control his impatience as the vessel slowly chugged into the dock. In the dim light he could just make out his own name on the pilothouse. It was the *John J. Healy,* one of his own company's boats.

Healy raced up the gangplank as soon as it was laid down. He was greeted on deck by Ely Weare, the son of the president of the company. Healy at once asked what cargo the ship brought. Weare proudly told him that it was loaded with as much whisky and hardware as the boat could transport across the Yukon flats.

At these words, which meant there was little or no food aboard, Healy leaped at Weare in a blind fury, grasped him by the throat, and demanded to know why his instructions had been disobeyed. He had sent strict orders that the vessel was to bring nothing but food and clothing to beleaguered Dawson. He began to shake Weare like a rat, and might have killed him, but his assistant, a trained amateur boxer, pulled them apart. Weare shamefacedly replied that Charles Hamilton, in charge of the company's post at St. Michael, considered there was more money in liquor and hardware than there was in food.

When Hansen reached Dawson he found it in a desperate state. Soon the freeze-up would lock the town away from the world. His news—that the other boats were stuck in the shallow river four hundred miles away—brought the panic to a head.

Hansen strode up and down the main street making speeches warning those without adequate supplies to leave town at once and go down to Fort Yukon for the winter. "Go! Go! Flee for your lives!" he cried to the little crowds of sullen men gathering in the streets. Along the riverfront Hansen went from group to group, crying: "Go! Do you expect to catch grayling all winter?"

Sergeant Major Davis of the Mounted Police and Thomas Fawcett, the gold commissioner, also walked the streets urging the people to go while there was still time. Captain Charles Constantine, head of the police, posted notices along the river urging an immediate move out of town. "Starvation now stares everyone in the face who is hoping or waiting for outside relief," the notices read.

Then, as if by a miracle, two steamboats, the *Portus B. Weare* and the *Bella,* puffed into Dawson. Unfortunately they were only lightly loaded.

The *Weare,* it turned out, had been subjected to one of the most respectable armed hold-ups in history at Circle City. There were eighty miners left at Circle, without a scrap of food for the winter, when the ship docked briefly. The men asked permission to purchase a winter's outfit each. The captain refused. He was determined to get his cargo intact to Dawson. The men then held a meeting and decided to take their outfits by force.

Twelve of them with loaded Winchester rifles kept the crew at bay while the others unloaded eighty outfits from the boat. These were taken immediately to the company store, where each man paid the storekeeper in cash for his goods. The storekeeper in his turn then paid each of the hold-up men longshoreman's wages for unloading the boat!

The situation at Dawson now seemed so desperate that the *Weare* dropped its passenger fare to fifty dollars a head to encourage men to leave town for the winter. Then it headed out in a race with winter for St. Michael. The government decided to offer free passage on the *Bella* to anyone who would leave town and winter at Fort Yukon. One hundred and sixty people took advantage of the offer, and the little boat headed downriver under full steam as the blocks of ice began to drift down the river.

Neither steamboat reached its destination. Both were caught in the ice before reaching Fort Yukon. Eighty passengers from the *Weare* pushed on through the ice floes in small boats. The ice froze around them, imprisoning the boats, and they kept on on foot. For three days they walked through the freezing forests without food. They arrived finally at Fort Yukon, cold, hungry, and destitute, only to find that this settlement too was short of food. Once again men took the law into their own hands. They seized the Alaska Commercial Company's cache at gunpoint and insisted on outfits for the winter. A squad of U. S. militia was powerless to stop them. The government backed down and allowed them to take what they needed.

All this time, with the river thick with sluggishly moving ice, the last of the stampeders had been inching their way down the river on hastily built boats and rafts, determined to reach the Klondike before freeze-up. One gray October day the hungry watchers on the Dawson shoreline watched a raft loaded with meat sweep helplessly past the city. A man on board shouted into the wind that he would pay a thousand dollars to any man who could reach him with a line. But he was too far out in the stream. The raft swept on and was wrecked fourteen miles downriver. The following day the ice jammed in front of the town, the blocks freezing together at strange and awkward angles, crushing the last of the boats between them as they froze. Dawson was locked in.

As the ice ground to a stop, a pall of melancholy settled over the town, accentuated by a variety of mournful sounds—the creaking and crunching of the ice blocks, the weird whining of hundreds of dogs, the eerie screaming of the black ravens that hovered and fluttered above in the gray skies like death-watchers. Men, bewildered, sullen, and discontented, gathered in the streets, solemn and speechless, wondering what to do next. Four hundred of them held a mass meeting and decided to risk a trip over the ice, upriver to the passes. They set out a short time later, some with dogs, some dragging their sleds by hand. Eventually most of them reached Skagway or Dyea, but not without terrible hardships that made the amputation of men's fingers, legs, and arms necessary because of frostbite and gangrene.

Dawson settled down to a long, hungry winter. It was ironic that all over the north country men were clawing their way up frozen rivers and down forest trails and over mountain passes in tens of thousands to reach this town and the riches it contained. But in the town itself all the money in the world could not have bought a Christmas turkey. The following April, when a Dutchman brought a turkey in over the trail, ready cooked and stuffed, it was exhibited as an oddity in the Pioneer Saloon. Raffled off, it fetched one hundred seventy-four dollars.

By midwinter Dawson was down to essentials. Only one man in town had fresh potatoes left, and he saved them for special occasions. Dried potatoes sold for a dollar a pound. The police went on reduced rations and refused to arrest anybody unless he had his own provisions to take to jail with him. It didn't matter greatly. There was no chance of escape from Dawson anyway.

At one point the entire menu stock in the lunch counter of the M and M Saloon consisted of a bottle of Worcestershire sauce, some tins of milk, a few sardines, a pan of beans, and a loaf of bread. A meal of beans, stewed apples, and bread in the Eldorado Café cost three dollars and fifty cents—about ten times what it would cost in Vancouver. Before the winter was over, the restaurants had closed their doors.

Flour grew scarcer and scarcer, and the prices soared from fifteen dollars a sack to seventy-five dollars. Greedy men hoarded their supplies, hoping for a price rise. One man had one hundred and eighty sacks and turned down offers of seventy-five dollars a sack, holding out for one hundred dollars. Alas for him, the prices began to drop again as a general unloading of hoarded provisions took place in the spring. Flour was soon back at its old price.

The news of Dawson's starvation winter caused a flurry of concern in the outside world. This led, finally, to a ludicrous relief expedition being formed. The U. S. Congress voted a sum for the purchase of 539 reindeer in Lapland to be herded into Dawson as live meat. These animals were accompanied by 114 Lapps and Finns. But, sad to say, it was the relief expedition that, in the end, required relief. As the starvation winter drew to a close and the sun began to melt the river ice and the boats began to ready themselves for another season, the wretched reindeer themselves died of starvation.

CHAPTER 7

THE TERRIBLE CHILKOOT PASS

WHILE DAWSON STARVED, MEN STRUGGLED.

All over the north, in twos and threes, in sixes and sevens, alone and in masses of thousands, they struggled to cross the various mountain divides which bar the Yukon country from the outside world.

All told, they numbered something like one hundred thousand, scattered from the Arctic to Ashcroft, B.C. But by far the largest numbers were slowly making their way over the slippery trail that led from Dyea on the seacoast up the terrible Chilkoot Pass and into the lake country at the headwaters of the Yukon.

Of all the routes that led to the Klondike, the Chilkoot was the most famous and the most popular. Strenuous and heart-breaking as it was, it turned out in the end to be the best way to reach the land of gold. Between the fall of 1897 and the spring of 1898, twenty-two thousand men had climbed in single file up the steps of ice and into the blizzards that almost ceaselessly swept the summit of the pass. After more than half a century, the wreckage of that memorable climb—bottles, old packs, twisted cable, lumber, torn sleeping bags—is still to be seen, lying among the ice-shrouded boulders. But few see it, for nobody crosses the Chilkoot anymore.

The trail to the Chilkoot began at the town of Dyea, Skagway's twin neighbor on the seacoast. From here it led up a wooded river valley in a series of easy ascents toward the base of the mountain barrier. It led through a dizzy canyon, along a strip of pleasant woods, and thence upward through the mountains. Along this trail several roaring little cities sprang up, where as many as five thousand men were camped at a single time. There was Canyon City at the canyon, and Pleasant Camp in the woods, and finally Sheep Camp, the biggest of all, at the base of the mountain ascent.

Here, pitched in the deep snow, were thousands upon thousands of tents, and tons upon tons of supplies were piled in helter-skelter hillocks. Sheep Camp was the halfway station between Dyea and the summit of the Chilkoot. Here the timber ended. Beyond this point no tree could grow.

The camp lay in a round valley at the end of the canyon and

was named Sheep Camp because, before the rush, it had been the headquarters for mountain-sheep hunters. All around it loomed the great sawtooth mountains. In one of these mountains a deep notch could be seen. This was the Chilkoot Pass.

The camp's population shifted daily. Part of it was made up of men who had succeeded in moving their outfits this far from the seacoast. Part was made up of men lugging their supplies piecemeal the rest of the way to the summit. The remainder were professional packers, gamblers, saloon-keepers, restaurant men, and birds of prey.

Here at the Broadway Eating House a man could buy a sparse meal of bacon, beans, and tea for two dollars and fifty cents. In the Palmer Hotel, a single frame room twenty by forty feet, men slept on the floor so thickly that there was no room left to walk. A brook running through one corner of the room served as a washbasin in the morning.

In the fall of 1897, as the snow commenced to fall, Sheep Camp was a bedlam of sweating men, howling dogs, and abandoned horses. The horses roamed everywhere without masters. For no horse, no matter how sure-footed, could make the terrible climb that faced every man on the Dyea Trail. These wretched creatures, cut adrift by their masters, hobbled about the camp, their backs raw from wet blankets, their legs cut and bruised on rocks, thin and starving, stumbling onto and into tents, tripping on guy ropes, seeking food, shelter, and companionship. In the end they were all rounded up and shot and their bodies buried quickly under the swiftly falling snow. All winter the snow continued to fall. It lay so thick that no man knew how far below him the ground was. In midwinter one party punched a hole in the snow with a pole to try to test the depth. The pole went down seven feet before it hit bottom. "Bottom" was a dead horse.

Four miles above Sheep Camp lay another miniature city called The Scales. This was the beginning of the pass, and here men weighed their goods. Packers' prices increased from this point on. Men with money could avail themselves of the services of the packers or of an aerial tramway, a cable-and-pulley arrangement which hauled men's goods to the summit. But by far the majority carried all their property—from whipsaws to sleds—on their backs.

Here were piled thousands of tons of freight. And from this point to the top of the pass all day long could be seen a solid moving line of black. The picture of this line of men, toiling ever upward like ants, is the most famous of all the Gold Rush photographs. If the great stampede had a focal point, this was it.

One behind another, without a gap between, the men labored up the thousand-foot pass. The angle was forty-five degrees, so steep that a man had to bend only slightly to touch the snow ahead of him. This last climb took an average of six hours of steady trudging. The climbers were aided by steps cut into the ice and a rope alongside. There were fifteen hundred of these steps, and the effect was as if a man set out to climb an enormous slippery staircase with a fifty- or hundred-pound load on his back—a staircase that seemed to have no end.

There was no let-up in this steady ascent, if you were bent on reaching the summit and returning to Sheep Camp before dark. There were occasional seats cut in the side of the icy trail, but if a man stepped out of the ever-moving human chain it might be hours before he could find a gap and get back in place. And so each man struggled on, trying not to groan aloud, each face purple with strain, each pair of lungs bursting with effort. Occasionally a man would fall to the ground weeping with fatigue. The line of men would slowly pass him by without a murmur.

On the summit, where blizzards blew remorselessly, each man's goods were piled up in small mountains. There were thousands of these piles, with paths threading in between them, so that the summit, at a casual glance, looked like a miniature city. Occasionally the snow swept down so thickly that it covered this city of provisions. Many owners were unable to find their goods again before spring. By March there were three layers of these "cities" under seventy feet of snow.

The trip back to The Scales was as swift as the ascent was slow. The stampeders slid down the mountain in a matter of minutes. The thousands of sliding men wore a deep chute in the ice, as deep as the walls of a room. A man ready to descend simply jumped into the chute, kicked his feet out, and shot to the bottom in a ball of snow, jumping up quickly to get out of the way of the next man.

This was the scene all that winter: a mountain alive with men, like a great snow-covered anthill. It was a scene never repeated.

On the Skagway Trail thousands more men were toiling across the White Pass. The White Pass was considerably lower than the Chilkoot, but the trail was fifteen miles longer. There was not a great deal to choose between them. A man standing at the top of Porcupine Hill and looking back along the trail toward Skagway could see nothing but men and sleds solidly packed together for two miles. From Porcupine Hill to the summit of the pass there were no steps cut in the ice, nor was there any level place to sit. The trail was so narrow that two men could scarcely pass each other.

Bert Parker, the seventeen-year-old boy from Ontario, struggled along the White Pass Trail with the others. He compared the line of moving men to a chain gang and the trail to a slippery pipeline. The men's feet had packed the snow hard so that it did not blow away, and as more snow fell and was packed down, the trail began to rise above the surrounding countryside until it was several feet higher. Parker watched as men beside him slipped off into the soft snow, often plunging in up to their waists. "If a man forgets for a moment what he is doing, his sled is liable to get off the trail and upset in the snow," young Bert wrote. "The minute this happens the man behind him steps up and takes his place and he stays there until the whole cavalcade passes by, which may take four or five hours. Sometimes you would think a man had gone crazy when his sled upset off the trail."

On the trip from the White Pass summit to the lakes the crush was even worse. Here were two narrow lanes of traffic and a black line of moving men as far as the eye could see. Men passed so close together their elbows brushed. This narrow trail continued for eight miles, and all along the route were tons of provisions dropped by men who came so far and then hurried back for another load. Mixed with the stacked outfits was the wreckage left behind by men who could no longer stand the hardships and had returned home, leaving their outfits behind them: broken sleds, abandoned tackle, heaps of camp refuse, discarded clothing.

Over these two trails, from Dyea and Skagway through the mountains to the lakes, men packed everything under the sun. Early in 1897, Billy Huson, a musician, and his wife packed the first piano over the Chilkoot. It was carefully dismantled and the sounding-board wrapped in wool yarn, which Mrs. Huson later knitted into sweaters and sold at a profit in Dawson. The piano was sold to Harry Ash of the Northern Saloon for twelve hundred dollars.

Captain A. J. Goddard and his wife packed two steamboats and a sawmill in sections over the two passes. Captain Goddard was an old steamboat man and his wife was a pilot. He had the boats built so they could be dismantled and fitted together again. He took his steamboat down to Dawson in the spring, through three sets of rapids, and became the first man to do so.

One man who made the most of his experience was a Swedish immigrant photographer named E. A. Hegg. His sled, with its built-in darkroom, pulled by six long-haired and sure-footed goats, became a familiar sight on the Dyea Trail. He took photographs and sold them as he went along. Later he built a boat, set up a tent in one corner, and floated down the Klondike. He had to filter his water through pieces of charcoal and heat his developing-fluid after it froze solid. But he made a graphic picture record of the great stampede. When one of his photographs went on display in a New York shopwindow, people fought one another for a sight of it and police had to be called to keep order.

Another who crossed the Chilkoot that winter was a young man in his twenties named Jack London. His pack was full of books: Darwin's *Origin of Species,* Spencer's *Philosophy of Style,* Marx's *Capital,* Milton's *Paradise Lost.* In the end this young man was to make himself rich, not from Klondike gold, but from novels which he wrote about the Klondike and the great stampede—*The Call of the Wild* and *White Fang*.

Although the average load for a man to carry was fifty pounds, there were some prodigious feats of strength seen along the trail that winter. One Indian packer took on his back a huge box which was weighed out at four hundred pounds at The Scales. Frederick Palmer, a newspaperman, saw a huge Swede crawl up the pass on his hands and knees with three giant six-by-four timbers strapped to his back.

There were many such scenes, some strange, some laughable, some dramatic, some tragic. Hamlin Garland wrote that he saw a flock of turkeys being driven over the White Pass by a one-armed man with a tam o'shanter on his head. The birds' feathers had long since blown away, and they were weary, disconsolate, and bewildered. One young boy crossed the Chilkoot with a heavy bundle of American newspapers. He sold them in Dawson for high prices and came out the following summer with his passage paid and two hundred fifty dollars to boot.

Children went over the passes with packs on their backs. Women struggled along under fifty-pound loads. Mont Hawthorne, who later wrote a book about his experiences, passed an aged German woman trudging through the snows in a long, full dress and a lace apron.

For every man who got through, there was one who turned

back. Jim Carroll, a former lightweight boxing champion, fell exhausted on the White Pass Trail and told his wife he could go no farther. "All right," she declared, "we'll split the outfit right here on the trail. I'm going on to Dawson." Rather than lose his wife, Carroll summoned up strength to go on. Later, in Dawson, they prospered: he gave boxing lessons, she opened a restaurant.

Terrible scenes took place on the trails during that terrible winter, but most of them passed unheeded. Arthur Walden, the mail carrier, reported that he saw a dead man with the back of his head smashed in lying beside the Skagway Trail. Scores of men passed this grisly cadaver, but none paid it any attention. All were obsessed with a fixed idea: push on to the Klondike, no matter what the cost.

Another wretched man lay all day on the Dyea Trail with a broken leg and no man would lift a hand to aid him. Finally Tom Linville, a professional packer, happened by. It was late in the evening and the man weighed one hundred and eighty pounds, but Linville picked him up and staggered with him on his back the full twenty-eight miles to Dyea. The two of them got there just as dawn was breaking.

Walden saw another fearful sight on the Skagway Trail. A weary stampeder had finally made it over the summit. Suddenly, half demented by fatigue, he turned in a rage upon his dogs. He began to flail at them with a club, slowly at first, then with greater vigor until he could no longer lift his arms. Finally, in a paroxysm of fury he began to push each animal under a waterhole in the ice until he had drowned his entire team. Only then did he realize the enormity of his actions. He sat down in the snow and began to sob.

Madness, sudden death, and suicide haunted the mountains that year. One stampeder from Oregon mortgaged his home and headed north with an outfit. It was washed away with the high tide at Skagway. Numbed by the loss, he came upon a cache of provisions with the owner asleep beside it. He killed the sleeper with a pick and buried the body in the sand. Yet, try as he might, he could not seem to get one of the dead man's hands completely covered. Finally he left with the stolen goods, forever haunted by the memory of that dead hand pointing accusingly from the shallow grave. Years later he went mad and was confined to an insane asylum, where he kept crying over and over again: "The hand! The hand!"

Yet it would not be fair to suggest that all the men who trod the trail that winter fell prey to avarice or panic. The excitement of the quest and the weariness of the course certainly drove many to abnormal excesses. But others still found time and energy to exercise the fundamental human decencies. Young Bert Parker, violently ill from eating rotten horsemeat on the White Pass, was pulled out of the storm by a stranger who cared for him in his tent for two days while a blizzard raged outside. Most men who crossed the passes could tell similar tales.

The sneak thief was held in contempt by all. Theft was an even greater crime than murder that winter. A man who stole from a comrade was looked upon with loathing and disrespect. One who stole was strapped to a tree and flogged with a rope. Another was sent back to the seacoast. He was forced to carry a heavy bedroll under one arm and was followed by an armed man on horseback who would not let him stop to rest or shift his load.

The trails held another pitfall. Mingling with the bona-fide gold-seekers were suave-looking confidence men with dummy packs full of feathers. Here and there on the trail they set up crooked games of chance, stripping the luckless cheechakos of whatever funds they had.

Almost all of these men were part of an enormous army of thieves, cutthroats, and cardsharps recruited and ruled by Jefferson Randolph Smith, a moon-faced, bearded rogue of great cunning who bore the nickname of "Soapy" and eventually made himself dictator of Skagway.

Soapy Smith's rule continued until his dramatic death on July 8, 1898. Just four days before, riding a magnificent white horse, he had led the Independence Day parade down the town's main street. But a group of citizens, goaded to the point of revolt by his barefaced tactics, held a protest meeting on one of the wharfs. They posted a cool, straight-shooting civil engineer named Frank Reid as a guard while they decided on the best way of ridding Skagway of its crooked element.

Down the street came Soapy Smith, gun in hand, determined to break up the meeting. Reid challenged him, Soapy tried to seize his gun, and both men fired together. Each fell to the dock. Soapy had died instantly, shot between the eyes. Reid lingered for ten days, then he too died. The citizens rounded up more than sixty desperadoes and swiftly sent them packing. Thus ended the strange rule of Jefferson Randolph Smith.

Before the great rush had spent itself in the heat of a new summer, a terrible tragedy struck the Chilkoot Pass. It was the second of two disasters. The first had occurred in the fall of 1897. Hanging over the pass like a brooding white monster was a giant glacier that held locked in its embrace a miniature lake. One day a piece of the glacier fell away and tons of water descended on the pass, engulfing everything, drowning the men in its path, and pushing giant boulders about like marbles.

The second disaster, on April 3, 1898, was far worse. For several weeks the stampeders had been warned of the dangers of snowslides and avalanches as the sun began to soften the great ledges of snow that hung over the peaks. The professional packers and experienced climbers used to sleep by day and climb by night, when the temperature dropped and the trails were frozen. But many refused to heed the warnings, and a large number insisted on using a cut-off trail that led to slightly easier climbing, though it was considered unsafe.

Then one day a party of men came hurrying down this trail, crying to the climbers to flee for their lives—an avalanche was coming. It was too late. An enormous wall of snow thundered down the slopes, burying everybody. Sixty-eight men lost their lives, smothered in strange twisted positions as the snow fell in tons upon them.

Within fifteen minutes of this disaster there were fifteen hundred rescuers on the scene digging with frantic haste to save those below the snow who were slowly suffocating. Seven living men were exhumed in this manner, but three of them were so far gone that they expired before nightfall.

This bitter April day was the climax of the Chilkoot rush. By now thousands of men were up and over the pass and sledding their goods down a chain of small lakes to the two large inland lakes of Bennett and Lindemann. Here the Yukon River rises in the green glacial waters, and here thousands upon thousands of gold-seekers were putting together the crude boats that would soon sweep in a mighty flotilla down the cold Yukon to the goldfields of the Klondike.

CHAPTER 8

A THOUSAND TRAILS LED NORTH

SUPPOSE SOMEONE HAD TAKEN A SET OF PINS and stuck them into a map of the northwest in the winter of 1897–98. Suppose each pin represented a gold-seeker headed for the Klondike. From the Arctic Ocean to the southern part of British Columbia the map would be almost solid with pins.

There would be clusters of pins running up the Yukon River all the way from the Bering Sea to Dawson. These pins would represent men aboard steamboats striving vainly to reach Dawson and locked for the season in the ice.

There would be pins of course at Dyea, Skagway, Lake Bennett, and Lake Lindemann, and there would be pins all the way down to the Klondike between these points. These pins would represent more men frozen into the ice aboard self-built rafts and scows.

There would be pins all the way up the Mackenzie River to the Arctic Circle. There would be pins all along the Rocky Mountains between the Mackenzie and Yukon rivers. There would be pins up the Peel and the Wind rivers and on the Rat and the Bell and the Porcupine, all far to the north of Dawson City.

There would be pins studded all the way up through British Columbia to Teslin Lake, which joins the Yukon by means of the Teslin River, and there would be pins all through the Peace River country, down the swift Liard, along the Pelly divide, and at the headwaters of the Stewart. There would, indeed, be close to one hundred thousand pins, each representing a man fighting against the snow and the mountains, the cold and the wind, and the weight of his ton of provisions—and all scattered over an area larger than the continent of Australia.

For there was no single "Trail of Ninety-Eight," as some people suppose. There were thousands of trails. Apart from the Dyea and Skagway trails, the gold-seekers followed three major routes.

One was the water trail that led by ship up the seacoast to the mouth of the Yukon and thence upriver to the Klondike.

One was the interior route which led up through the heart

of British Columbia to Teslin Lake in the Yukon and thence down the Teslin River to the Yukon River.

One was the "Edmonton route" which led from Edmonton toward the Mackenzie River and fanned out like the branches of a tree into trails that led over the mountains and into the Yukon all the way from the Peace River to the Arctic.

All these routes proved far less effective than the Chilkoot and White passes. Of the men who rushed to the Yukon in 1897 by the other routes, not a single one reached Dawson before freeze-up and hardly more than a handful made it the following spring when the other stampeders poured down the Yukon River. Some men were more than two years on these other trails, and of the thousands who took them, the vast majority never reached their destination at all.

The trouble with the all-water route was that the river froze before the boats could reach Dawson. After the news of the Klondike strike broke, thousands stormed the ticket offices for passage north. But by the time the stampeders reached St. Michael at the river's mouth it was August and the water was low. Steamboats were stranded on shoals and sandbars all along the river for seventeen hundred miles. And there they stayed with their frustrated passengers for eight long, cold months. The all-water route, in short, took almost a year.

There were two main routes through British Columbia.

One led up from Ashcroft over an overgrown trail that had not been used for a generation. This trail was cut out of the wilderness in 1865 in the days when Western Union, the great telegraph company, planned to join Russia and North America by cable. The cable was to go up through British Columbia, the Yukon, and Alaska, but the successful laying of the Atlantic cable ended the project.

Up through the matted underbrush of this forgotten pathway cut through the black pines, the Klondikers plodded. At times the trail was almost indistinguishable and only the rusted and twisted cable along the way gave a clue to the route. Here and there a dead horse showed that other men had gone before.

Finally the plodders reached the country of the majestic but treacherous Skeena River and the terrible Skeena swamp. The swamp was all but impassable for horses. Half of the animals who entered its dark confines, with its bottomless mudholes, its moss-enshrouded trees, and its dark, dripping evergreens, never came out. Here in this silent, gloomy world many men turned back and cursed the day they ever set out for the Klondike.

The men who pushed on reached Glenora at the head of navigation on the Stikine River. Here they joined the men who had pushed up the Stikine from Wrangell on the seacoast. At one point there were five thousand stampeders camped at

Glenora in tents and shacks, hoping to cross the mountains into the Teslin country and boat their way down to the Yukon.

The Stikine route had proved a virtual failure. A railway had been promised along this route into the Teslin country. Men had actually bought tickets, but not a tie was ever laid. The winter trail had been such hard going that many men had thrown away half their goods. Wet slush made traveling so difficult that only the lightest loads got through. By spring the entire country was a great marsh and starving men were beating their dogs to death and boiling and eating them.

Glenora was really only the start. There was almost a thousand more miles of traveling ahead over the mountains and down the rivers to the Klondike. Seven thousand men started up the Stikine route to the Yukon. Fewer than half made it.

It was considered patriotic for Canadians to use these various "All-Canadian" routes. Boards of trade in Edmonton, Victoria, and Vancouver praised them highly. Arthur Heming, a well-known artist and woodsman of the day, boosted the old fur-traders' route. This led north from Edmonton to Athabasca Landing and thence down to the Mackenzie River and almost to the Arctic. From here the route led over the divide by way of the Peel, the Rat, the Bell, and the Porcupine rivers to the Yukon River. From this point the weary men were supposed to pole their boat more than four hundred miles upriver to Dawson.

Heming called the route—it was twenty-five hundred miles long—"the inside track" and announced that it was "ridiculously cheap."

"All you need," he wrote, "is a good constitution, some experience in boating and camping, and $150." He added that by this route the Klondike could be reached in two months.

It is estimated that about two thousand men and a few women started out from Edmonton on variations of this trail. Hundreds turned back and hundreds more—perhaps five hundred—died en route. Of the handful that finally did reach the Klondike two years later, all were in rags and close to starvation. Most of them took passage aboard the first steamer and left the north forever.

But Edmonton benefited. The town swelled in size from a few hundred to four thousand. Every building was crammed, and hundreds of tattered tents and bivouacs ringed the city. The streets were full of ponies, the saloons ran wide open, and scattered shots peppered the night air.

A strange mélange of characters walked the streets. There was, for example, a party of titled and wealthy Englishmen under the leadership of Lord Avonmore. The townspeople called him Lord Have-One-More because he drank so much. The party's enormous outfit included several gross of toilet paper and fifty cases of champagne.

The streets were full of curious contrivances—little carts,

cabooses, and sleds to be pulled over slippery muskeg. One party from Chicago had built a steam-driven sleigh. The driving-wheel was a steel drum from which spikes projected to give it traction. The sleigh was christened the "I Will" at an elaborate ceremony. It set off for the Klondike amid cheers, its furnace roaring, steam hissing, and black smoke pouring from its funnel. It moved exactly one hundred yards, digging deeper into the black muck at every revolution. Finally it gave up for good. The "I Will" just wouldn't.

Texas Smith, another stampeder, had invented a machine called "The Duck." It was a strange contraption of axles put through wooden wine barrels. This was supposed to take the Duck across muskeg, high ground, ice, and snow, and at first it worked very well. But the hoops soon began to come off the barrels, and before it had gone three miles the whole thing suddenly collapsed. Texas Smith went back to Texas.

Some of the stampeders went straight north from Edmonton to the Mackenzie River country. Others went northwest to the rolling Peace River land. From the Peace they hoped to make their way to the Yukon along the same general route now taken by the Alaska Highway. Few are on record as having succeeded.

The Peace River country belonged to the Indians, and no white man had a legal right to enter it in 1898. Most Klondikers abused the natives. One group found its horses being killed unwittingly in Indian bear traps. As a result they destroyed every trap they found. They lived to regret this action. The Indians charged them by surprise one morning a few days later and destroyed everything they owned.

Yet some good came from all this effort, for this was the start of the rich farmland which now lies along either side of the broad Peace. Those Klondikers who didn't turn back stayed in the country and established homesteads in the rolling hills. Their great grandsons, many of them, are wealthy Peace River farmers today.

All this while, hundreds more men were working their way along the water routes that led to the Arctic. There were so many of them that a traveler arriving back in Edmonton in the spring of 1898 reported that he'd passed a solid line of boats the whole length of Lesser Slave Lake, for seventy-five miles.

The tiny Hudson's Bay Company forts along the way soon mushroomed into small cities. Athabasca Landing, for example, jumped from a population of fifty to one thousand. But every conceivable hazard lay before the gold-seekers. The rapids on the Athabasca and Slave rivers seemed unending. There were the Grande Rapids, the Burnt Rapids, the Drowned Rapids, the Middle Rapids, the Long Rapids, the Boiler Rapids, and the Cascade Rapids. These last rapids consisted of a sheer drop of as much as twelve feet over a limestone ledge. At one point the stampeders had to take their boats out of the water and haul them overland around sixteen miles of fast water.

By the time the argonauts had reached Fort Simpson on the Mackenzie, their numbers had thinned and many were cursing Arthur Heming, the artist who said the trip could be made in two months. Heming had neglected one significant point. The old *coureurs de bois* of the Hudson's Bay Company had indeed made the journey in two months. But they had traveled in fast canoes paddled by Indian helpers, and they had traveled light. They carried letters of credit on the great fur company and bought their provisions from each trading-post as they required them. The Klondikers, on the other hand, had no help and each one carried more than a ton of supplies.

The hardier ones pressed on down the Mackenzie. By now it was the summer of 1898 and many had been traveling since the previous fall. They still had thousands of miles to go and only a short time left to navigate the river.

Those in the vanguard reached the great Mackenzie delta near the Arctic before the freeze-up caught them. Here the river splits into dozens of channels before it joins the Arctic Ocean. The land is dreary and dark, the spruce trees are stunted, the islands depressingly flat, the riverbanks slippery with soft mud. Another huge river comes down through the mountains to join the Mackenzie just above the delta. This is the Peel. Up this waterway the stampeders turned. They were now eighteen hundred miles north of Edmonton, and the Klondike lay hundreds of miles to the southwest.

The exhausted men began to drag their boats up the tributaries of the Peel, seeking the various mountain divides that separate the Mackenzie watershed from the Yukon. Some went up the Rat River and others up the Wind, their eyes on the snowy mountains ahead.

Already the weather had turned bitterly cold. No longer could the men sit in their flatboats and let the current carry them along. Now they were working against the current. Each party had to "track" its boat up the rivers, which grew narrower and swifter and shallower as they went.

Tracking is a crude form of towing, and it is perhaps the hardest work in the world. The boat crews fixed lines to the bow of their craft and spaced themselves along the rope. Each man had a canvas sling over his shoulder with a knot that could easily be undone. Through this he slipped his head and one arm. Then he pulled the sling over his shoulder. The sling had to be loose enough so he could duck out of it quickly, for if the steersman in the boat slipped, the pull of the current could yank the entire crew off the bank into the water.

There was, of course, no towpath along these banks. Men plunged along over fallen trees, up cliffs, and through prickly shrubs. Sometimes they walked in the river itself, stumbling from rock to rock and pulling the heavily loaded boat behind them.

As winter came on, the watery path grew more and more difficult and more and more men turned back. Now the crews were all plunging along in the shallow water. It was so cold that men's legs broke out in boils. At night they went to sleep in drenched clothing, and in the morning, when they awoke, their clothing was still wet.

By freeze-up a handful had got over the mountains, but most were sealed up in this lonely, unexplored land for eight months of winter. They huddled together for companionship in crude cabins clustered together into tiny makeshift "cities" on the headwaters of the various streams that tumbled down from the passes.

One group wintered at the head of the rapids on the Rat River in a melancholy collection of tents and huts called Destruction City. The name was apt, for here the snarls of wreckage marked the failure of scores of men to navigate the fast water.

Another group spent the winter at Wind City on the Wind River. Scurvy swept this settlement, and more than three quarters of the men suffered from it. Their legs swelled up and their ribs bulged out like barrel hoops. Ten percent of the men died, and because the ground was frozen their corpses were stuffed down an empty mineshaft. When the shaft was full, the remainder of the bodies were wrapped in blankets and set out on tree platforms, Indian style, to keep off wild animals. Many who did not die suffered terribly from gangrene. One man had to have his toes cut off to save his life. There were, of course, no surgical instruments or anesthetics. His friends performed the operation with a hacksaw while he watched.

Here the men waited and rotted until the spring of 1899. Then most returned the way they had come without ever seeing the Klondike. A handful had got over the mountains the previous fall before freeze-up but these men still had not reached the Klondike. They had gone down the swift Bell River to the Porcupine and down the ice-choked Porcupine to its juncture with the Yukon. Here the freeze-up overtook them, four hundred miles from their goal. Some finally caught the spring steamers into Dawson. Others died in their cabins. In the spring of '99 a traveler walked into a stiff little tent outside Fort Yukon and came upon a grisly sight: here sat two dead men, frozen solid. In front of them was a pair of partly cooked moccasins sitting in a solid cake of ice in a kettle suspended over a heap of ashes. They had spent two years on this trail from Edmonton, vainly seeking Klondike gold, and this was their tragic reward.

CHAPTER 9

THE GREAT ARMADA DOWN THE YUKON

WHILE MANY MEN WERE STILL IN THE EARLY stages of the various inland trails, most of the stampeders who went by way of Skagway and Dyea were already across the passes. The early months of 1898 found them clustered by the thousands along the margins of the two slender lakes, Lindemann and Bennett, which mark the headwaters of the navigable Yukon.

The men crossing the Chilkoot proceeded down the slopes across a series of small lakes to Lake Lindemann. Some of them stopped here and commenced building boats. Others went farther along to Lake Bennett, where the White Pass empties out. At both places were canvas camps with thousands of tents whitening the shoreline.

Bennett, with a population exceeding ten thousand, was the largest tent city in the world. The tents and the cabins lined the lakeshore in a double row. Here were hot-bath emporiums, barber shops, saloons, and restaurants, mining agents, land agents, lawyers, doctors, dentists, and promoters, all doing a roaring business.

The entire lake was a bedlam of noise and energy. Smoke rose from thousands of campfires and cast a pale smog over the town. The air was alive with the crash of trees falling, the ring of saw and hammer, the whine of the mills, and the loud cursing of men. You could, if you wished, buy a boat for between two hundred fifty and six hundred dollars, but most men had no money and built their own.

The boat-builders were strung out for twenty-six miles along the lakeshore, from the foot of the passes to the Indian town of Caribou Crossing. The men presented a bizarre sight. Almost every one had a ragged beard. Their cheeks were sunken and their clothing tattered from the months of toiling over the passes. To keep the fierce ice glare from peeling their skin, they had daubed their faces with black charcoal. A stranger coming among them might easily have mistaken them for savage creatures from another world.

These men were whipsawing logs into planks from which they would build the flat-bottomed scows which most

Klondikers favored to transport themselves and their supplies downriver.

This whipsawing was so arduous that it caused the dissolution of scores of partnerships and often near-murders. Before the logs could be turned into planks, a saw pit had to be built. This was an elevated platform, ten or twelve feet high, on which each log was laid. One man stood on the platform and the other below. Between them they held the saw and commenced to saw the log into inch-thick boards. All the cutting was done on the downward stroke. Then the man below had to shove the saw up through the log to the man above. Terrible arguments resulted. The man above would claim that his partner below wasn't putting his weight into the saw. The man below would retort hotly that, on the contrary, *he* was doing all the work. At the end of six hours of whipsawing, both partners would be exhausted and angry. Often partnerships split up on the spot and the men divided their outfits. So bitter did some become that when something could not be divided, such as a boat, an ax, a tent, or a stove, it would literally be hacked in two and each man would go his own way, carrying his useless half with him.

As the work went on, constables of the Northwest Mounted Police moved through the crowds of sweating men, urging: "Build strong. Don't build a floating coffin." Without the redcoats present, chaos might easily have reigned. Early in the game a group of would-be real estate men had staked the shores of both lakes. They planned to charge every boat-builder two dollars a head for working there. The police soon sent them packing.

Now the constables were checking every boat before the long river journey. Besides a name, usually that of a wife, daughter, or girlfriend, every man was required to paint a number on his boat and every man had to check with the police before setting off down the Yukon. There were checkpoints, manned by the redcoats, every twenty-five miles down the river. If a man didn't turn up at a checkpoint, the police would know he was missing and a party would be sent out to search for him. In this way the Northwest Mounted kept disaster to a minimum.

By May the boats lay five and six deep for miles along the lakeshores. Forests of masts sprang up, each mast topped by a bandanna or a towel as a flag. As the ice began to recede from the shore, men launched their boats to the accompaniment of cheers. An air of expectancy hung over the lake.

Boats began to pour through the narrow rapids between Lindemann and Bennett as everybody poised himself for the break-up of the river below and the rush to Dawson. But for many these rapids held bitter disaster. Many boats were swamped in them and entire outfits lost. On the bank above was the grave of a man who had shot himself in despair because he had come so far and worked so hard only to lose his entire worldly possessions in this way.

On May 30 the ice broke. Immediately the gold-seekers hoisted their sails and pushed off. There were eight hundred craft launched that first day, a strange and awkward flotilla. Most of the boats were constructed of green spruce planks whipsawed from newly cut trees and caulked with flour bags boiled in spruce pitch.

Within a day or two the entire lake was dotted with these homemade sailboats moving with the gentle wind toward the Klondike. It was a dramatic and quite lovely scene. The high blue mountains dropped straight down to the glassy green waters of the lake, their snowy, sunlit peaks reflected in the perfect mirror of the water. In the boats the men were singing and laughing and calling cheerfully to one another. The long months of struggle in the passes and on the saw pits were ended. Now it was virtually smooth sailing for five hundred miles to Dawson City. The weather was warm—almost tropical by now—and it was pleasant to lie back in the stern and let the breeze propel you forward, and to dream of gold along the creek beds of the Klondike.

Of all the dramatic scenes of the stampede, this was the one that young Bert Parker, the teenage boy who traveled the trail of '98, remembered most graphically. He and three others shoved off on June 1 from the shores of Lake Bennett in a boat containing two stoves, two tents, and three tons of provisions. They passed into Tagish Lake about six in the evening. There was a soft haze lying over the lake and not a breath of wind blowing. From his boat Bert Parker could see thousands of other craft becalmed on the lake. Across the still waters came the sounds of quartets singing in harmony. The boats began to pull over to the shoreline and the men to make camp for the night. The campfires flickered along the shoreline for miles.

"Here, the day before at Lake Tagish, I don't suppose there had been more than ten men at one time since Creation," Bert Parker wrote. "Everything was in its natural state. Then, on this June day in 1898 there were some ten to twenty thousand men on its shore. They left the next morning and they have never been back since at the same time. Nor has any similar crowd been there since that memorable day."

There were some strange craft on the lake that day. One man, for example, had a boat made from a hollow log. It had two sticks put out each way for oar locks. This weird vessel was pulling a log raft on which were piles of hay and several tethered horses.

Another boat was built by four men from New Orleans who had designed it in the fashion of a Mississippi sidewheeler. Instead of oars, each man had a crank which turned the two sidewheels. Two men turned while two rested. If they wanted to change direction, one man turned his crank forward and the other turned backward. But it was not a very successful invention.

Every man checked in at the Mounted Police post at Tagish at the end of the lake. In six weeks eighteen thousand men and six hundred women checked in here. The boats were lined up solidly for four miles awaiting their turn.

Customs duty had to be paid here by the Americans who had purchased their goods in the United States. The average duty ran to about twenty-five percent of the cost of an outfit. Blankets, seasonal clothing, and a hundred pounds of provisions were exempted. The police took a fairly broad view of this duty, judging every case on its merits. If a man had no money to pay, he could work it off by spending a few days on the woodpile.

The stampeders pressed on, through the weeds of Marsh Lake and then into the narrow river that leads to Miles Canyon and the rapids beyond.

Here was the greatest obstacle on the river trip. The canyon is a hundred feet wide and almost as deep. Its red rock walls rise sheer from the water. The river forces itself between these walls at the foot of a steep cliff. Halfway through, the water crashes against softer rock, and here it has gouged out a round basin into which it swirls with whirlpool force. Then it is forced once more into a gorge which narrows down to thirty feet so that the water is squeezed up into a crest four feet higher in the center than at the sides.

After the canyon, the stampeders entered the Squaw Rapids, full of huge jutting rocks. Then they sped around a sharp twist in the river and plunged on into the foaming Whitehorse Rapids. Altogether it was a five-mile run.

Many men perished in these rapids and more lost their outfits and boats. Experienced river pilots made big money taking boats through for men who had no river experience. One enterprising man named Norman MacCauley built wooden rails around the canyon and rapids. He had cars made to fit the rails, and these were pulled by horses. He charged three cents a pound to freight goods over this primitive railway and was soon a rich man. All the gold, in those days, wasn't on the Klondike.

Hardier men chanced the rapids. Some lost their lives. In the Whitehorse Rapids alone there were fifty deaths in the summer of 1898. Thousands more, however, got through safely with no more than a drenching. One lonely and morose Englishman went through without knowing it, deep in his own thoughts. Another went through cheerfully playing the bagpipes. A Norwegian went through in a bateau grinding a music box until a wave cut the melody short. One man took a scowload of cats through. The felines had caused a problem at the Tagish customs post because nobody knew what the duty on cats was. Finally they were classed as fur and their owner was charged a dollar apiece. In Dawson they each sold for an ounce of gold—sixteen dollars.

The river below the rapids was soon alive with boats for most of its length to Dawson. All along the banks were camped the Stick Indians, dirty, smoky, ragged, and sick-looking, smoking salmon and offering to buy anything and everything from the voyagers who passed by. They traded with passion, and the cry "How muchee? How muchee?" rang out across the silent hills and valleys.

By this time the entire countryside seemed to be on fire. The stampeders had left their campfires smoldering, and this carelessness touched off raging blazes in the tinder-dry woods from riverbank to hilltop until the whole land lay under a blanket of smoke.

The voyagers checked in at the Lake Laberge police post, then hoisted their sails and let the wind sweep them across the thirty miles of ice-choked waters. After the lake they entered the treacherous, twisting Thirtymile River. By July this section of the Yukon was lined with the wrecks of scows and barges, while dozens more boats lay stuck fast on the shoals and bars.

At Hootalinqua, where the Teslin joins the Yukon, more

stampeders joined the flotilla of boats. These were men who had come up through the Skeena and Stikine trails and wintered in the Teslin country.

A little farther on some of the men paused at a deserted trading-post that stood on the riverbank just above Five Finger Rapids. There was a two-year-old notice on the cabin door saying that the occupant had gone to Fortymile for provisions but would soon return. The name on the sign was not without significance. It read: "George W. Carmack."

The ever-present police were here, too, warning the stampeders to keep to the right on the way through Five Fingers. Here four great pillars of rock erupted from the narrowing channel, leaving five "fingers" of rushing water. The stampeders took the righthand channel, and all but a few of them emerged safely.

Soon the broad, muddy Pelly River joined the Yukon at the old Hudson's Bay Company fort of Selkirk. Down the Pelly poured more boats. These men had crossed the divide from Liard and the Mackenzie, and they were the vanguard of the rush from Edmonton. The Alaska Commercial Company had a post at Selkirk, but there was nothing to sell. Thousands of men camped in the woods at the juncture of the two rivers, but the starving men from the Pelly country were hard put to get an ounce of rations. Everybody hung on grimly to the precious provisions which had been brought so far at such effort.

From this point on it was not much more than a day's run to the Klondike. Eagerly the stampeders pushed on, keeping to the right of the river in case, by error, they should be swept right past the town of which they had heard so much.

For no one knew quite where Dawson was. Young Bert Parker, in his boat, began to stop and ask the woodcutters whom he spotted on the riverbank along the way. But he didn't get much satisfaction. One man would tell the boy it was just around the next bend. He'd pass a couple of bends without finding the city. Then another man on the shore would tell him that Dawson was a hundred miles farther on. All young Bert could do was to hug the right bank, which slowed down his speed.

Finally he swung around a rocky bluff and saw before him a sight he would remember all the rest of his life. Pouring into the Yukon, just ahead, was the famous Klondike, and sprawled over the hills and along the flats and up each river as far as the eye could see were the thousands upon thousands of tents, shacks, and cabins of Dawson City, the greatest boomtown in the world.

CHAPTER 10
STAMPEDE'S END

IN MAY 1898, DAWSON CITY, WHICH HAD SURvived starvation, now faced a new danger: flood. The frozen river began to rise alarmingly on May 6. If the ice broke and then jammed below the town, it would serve as a dam and the entire community might be swept away. Once again fear stalked Dawson as the townspeople watched the surface of the river rise to within two feet of the bank.

Meanwhile, word had been slowly seeping into the icelocked city of the excitement outside. Shortly after the ice broke, the cry of "Cheechako!" rang out from the waterfront and hundreds poured down to watch a boat heave into view above Klondike City with five men, a dog, and a sled aboard. The crowds followed the boat for a mile along the bank until it landed. Then they learned, to their disappointment, that the passengers had only come from the Stewart River, where they had been frozen in since the previous fall.

Shortly after this a green Peterborough canoe slid into the bank. It, too, contained old sourdoughs who had sledded over the ice from Lake Bennett. Lake Laberge, they reported, was still frozen and there were thousands along its shores waiting for the break-up.

A few more canoes slipped in from various upriver points. All contained men who had wintered along the river and were therefore well ahead of the main rush, together with a few hardy souls who had sledded their provisions down the river in order to reach Dawson ahead of their companions.

Some of these made high profits on the goods they brought with them. One of the earliest arrivals was a Seattle man who had several crates of eggs with him. He sold the eggs at eighteen dollars a dozen to the hungry Dawsonites, disposing of them all within an hour of his arrival. Almost all the thirty-odd boats that arrived during that first week contained eggs, so that by late May, Dawson's hunger was satisfied and the price was down to three dollars a dozen.

One of the early arrivals made a profit of five thousand dollars on ladies' hats. Another sold condensed milk at three dollars a tin. A third disposed of fifteen hundred pairs of boots at fifteen dollars a pair. He had paid $1.75 a pair in Montreal.

In this vanguard was Commissioner Walsh of the Northwest Mounted Police. He was the same man who had once accepted the surrender of Sitting Bull, the famous Sioux Indian Chief. Appointed Commissioner of the Yukon the previous year by the Canadian government, Walsh had failed to reach Dawson before freeze-up and had wintered on the river. He told the excited townspeople that the police at Tagish had already checked three thousand boats at Tagish and more were pouring through by the hour.

Small numbers of men were now arriving daily, but the great flood was yet to come. All the same, Dawson was changing. One of the first of the newcomers was an enterprising young man named Eugene Allen. He was bent on starting Dawson's first newspaper, and he had hurried along over the ice ahead of the rest of his company in order to do so. As his printing press hadn't arrived, he founded the paper as a bulletin and called it the *Klondike Nugget*. Within a day or so a second paper, the *Yukon Midnight Sun,* was established.

Now the flood, which all Dawson had been fearing, was unleashed upon the town. The ice had finally jammed below the city and the rising river swept over the banks, plunging the entire community under two to five feet of water. On June 5 the water subsided, leaving the city a sea of mud. On June 6 a man arrived in a boat bringing with him a two-week-old copy of a Seattle newspaper which gave the news of Admiral

Dewey's great victory over the Spanish fleet in Manila Bay. Crowds gathered in the streets to have the paper read aloud to them, and later that evening hundreds paid a dollar apiece to hear further readings in the Pioneer Hall.

Two days later the great armada from Lake Bennett began to pour into Dawson. Suddenly the river seemed to be alive with boats. Day and night they kept coming without a break—rafts, scows, canoes, flatboats, bateaus. Soon the boats were stretched along the waterfront for two solid miles, six deep, like junks in a Chinese river port. Within a month Dawson's population had leaped to eighteen or twenty thousand.

Day after day the boats poured in, in an endless parade. They brought hay and horses, goats and cattle, cats and dogs, roosters and oxen. They brought Australians, Englishmen, Japanese, South Africans, Frenchmen, and Negroes. They brought gamblers, adventurers, dance-hall girls, Salvation Army lassies, nurses and doctors, lawyers and druggists, murderers and thieves.

The tents went up by the thousands. They sprouted like soft white mushrooms in the black muck of the waterfront. They overflowed the Dawson swamps and spilled into Lousetown across the Klondike and from there across the Yukon to West Dawson. They blossomed out on the hills and benches that overlooked the town and they straggled by the hundreds along the trails that led up the Klondike to the creeks. And scattered everywhere, like tall four-legged monsters, were little log caches on stilts.

Still the boats kept coming. The sawmills ran day and night to turn out lumber for the buildings that were now popping up along Dawson's Front Street. Lots sold for as much as twenty thousand dollars apiece. Men were happy to pay seven hundred forty dollars for a hundred-pound keg of nails. Rents were sky high. Signor Gandolfo, an Italian, paid one hundred twenty dollars a month for exactly five feet of air space next to a theater. He covered it with canvas, opened a fruit stall, and made a fortune.

By July, Front Street was like a carnival midway. You could buy anything in the world in the space of four or five short blocks, including peanuts and pink lemonade. You could buy patent-leather shoes, yellow-backed novels, cheap jewelry, mastodon's tusks, ice cream, opera glasses, safety pins, German sausages, and fresh grapes. Never before had the laws of supply and demand worked in such dramatic fashion. Brooms, which were scarce, sold for fourteen dollars apiece. Winchester rifles, which were a glut on the market, were auctioned off for a dollar each.

Every creek had long since been staked, and many men, unable to find gold, were reduced to selling their possessions. Outfits were piled all along the riverbank with "For Sale" signs tacked to them. Here you could purchase clothes, furs, hats, moccasins, shoes, and meat. Just two months before, Dawson had been empty of provisions. Now she was glutted. There was no fixed price for anything. They changed day by day and from place to place.

Front Street was a sea of mud. Through the mud thousands of men trudged restlessly backward and forward while horse-drawn wagons dropped to their axles in the muck and the animals floundered and struggled. All around them, dozens of dogs snapped and snarled and fought. A Projectoscope flashed advertising messages on a huge screen on one of the buildings. Outside each of a dozen saloons and dance halls, men known as "spielers" raucously proclaimed through megaphones to the swirling crowd the advantages of their particular establishment. Inside, a dozen hastily recruited orchestras filled the bright summer night with a wild cacophony. A few doors away, on a raised open-air platform, the famous Oatley sisters, Lottie and Polly, danced and sang their way into small fortunes. In the same block Frank Slavin, the heavyweight boxing champion of Australia, took on and bested all comers.

Every day brought new incidents. Tom Chisholm, a saloonkeeper, bought the first cow in town for a thousand dollars and milked it himself on the sawdust floor of the Aurora Number One. He sold the milk for five dollars a mug, which was ten times the price of a glass of whisky. Another man had, with great difficulty, packed a crate of live chickens over the Chilkoot. He had them sitting in a box at the police barracks. Soon it became obvious that one was about to lay an egg. Crowds gathered to watch the incident. The egg became the first to be laid in Dawson and was sold for five dollars before the hen had finished cackling.

There were no sewers or garbage disposals in Dawson. By mid-summer the whole city was a fetid, reeking swamp. Malaria and typhoid epidemics swept over the city and men expired daily in Father Judge's hospital.

The town became so glutted with men that friends lost track of one another. Tents moved position daily; men had been known only by nicknames on the trail. Bulletin boards placed along the waterfront contained dozens of notices by men seeking lost partners. One man spent a week searching vainly for his friend. His searches were interrupted when he was recruited as pallbearer for the funeral of a man who had died of typhoid. To his horror, he discovered that the corpse was that of the missing man he had been seeking.

There was no coin or paper currency in Dawson that year, and it cost five dollars to cash a hundred dollar check. All transactions were carried out in gold dust. Every man had his poke of caribou or moosehide, and every store and saloon had its gold scales. Pure gold was worth sixteen dollars an ounce, but most men used the so-called commercial dust, which wasn't pure, being mixed with black sand. This was worth only eleven dollars at the bank, but was accepted as legal tender elsewhere. Some men cheated by slipping brass filings in with their gold. Crooked saloonkeepers retaliated by loading their scales, slipping half-dollars under the weights.

But Dawson was in no sense a lawless town, as Skagway was. It had none of the Wild West atmosphere associated with most frontier towns. Indeed, Dawson was probably the tamest mining camp in history. There was scarcely a murder or a theft, an almost unbelievable record for an area whose population has been estimated at somewhere between eighteen and forty thousand.

This was entirely due to the presence of the Northwest Mounted Police, who ruled the community with hands of iron. Some of the toughest men in the world roamed Dawson's muddy streets, but none was allowed to carry a gun. One of the hardest men of the American west, a former marshal from Dodge City, was ejected from a saloon simply for talking too loudly! He went out like a lamb, and when a constable asked him to hand over the gun he was carrying he obeyed meekly.

The Mounties were broad-minded. They allowed the gaming-houses—where thousands of dollars ran on the turn of a card—to operate full-blast day and night, six days a week, even though gambling was technically illegal throughout Canada. But on Sundays they closed them tight. Two constables stood watch over the big games, never interfering with the play, but at five minutes before midnight on Saturday they made a sign to the gamekeeper and without a murmur the entire establishment shut down.

Sunday was by law a day of rest in Dawson. No work of any kind could be performed, and if a man was caught splitting his own wood he was arrested. Punishments were simple but effective. For minor offenses a man was sentenced to work for so many days on the municipal woodpile. For major offenses he was given a "blue ticket," which meant he had to leave town at once, never to return.

In mid-June the first of the steamers frozen in all winter along the river arrived in Dawson. Others quickly followed. In the Seattle shipyards all the previous winter men had been frantically building steamboats by the dozen in order to pick up some of the lucrative river trade to the Klondike. Soon dozens of black-stacked sternwheelers were puffing into Dawson, loaded with merchandise and passengers. By freeze-up more than seventy-five steamers had arrived in town.

With the arrival of the steamer cargoes, new and more imposing buildings went up. Hotels were erected, where orchestras played for impeccably tailored guests. Men in Prince Albert coats, with diamond stickpins in their ties, and women in evening dress ate seven-course meals from tables covered with fine linen, sterling silver, and bone china. Within three months Dawson had changed from a rough log camp to a cosmopolitan city.

In July, Dawson's first two bona-fide tourists arrived. Almost everybody else had come to the Klondike to make money, but Edith Van Buren and Mary E. Hitchcock had simply come in the role of sightseers. Miss Van Buren was the niece of a President of the United States. Mrs. Hitchcock was the widow of a United States Admiral. Every year these two wealthy socialites visited some world capital—Paris, London, Rome, Hong Kong, Rio. This year, not unnaturally, they had come to Dawson City. With their arrival it might be said that Dawson, too, had arrived.

These two remarkable women brought an equally remarkable cargo, which ran to several tons. Their supplies included two Great Danes, a bowling alley, a movie projector, fifty live pigeons, several caged canaries, a parrot, a mandolin, a zither, several air mattresses, a phonograph, a hundred-pound music box, a coal-oil stove, and an ice-cream freezer. For the ladies insisted on living in the style to which they were accustomed.

This paraphernalia was housed in the largest tent ever brought into the Yukon. It was a circus marquee, seventy feet long and forty feet broad. It was so big that the ladies pitched a second, smaller tent inside it in order to be cozier. Here, in their tailored suits, starched collars, and silk ties, they entertained such Klondike social lions as Big Alec McDonald. Their costumes were rendered slightly incongruous, perhaps, by the loaded pistols and cartridge belts that they sometimes strapped around their ample hips, but their meals were impeccable. They feasted on anchovies, mock turtle soup, roast moose, potato balls, escalloped tomatoes, asparagus salad with French dressing, peach ice cream, chocolate cake, and French drip coffee. Dawson had come a long way since its starvation winter.

The Salvation Army looked longingly at the big tent, which was pitched across the Yukon River from the main town, and asked to borrow it for Sunday services. The ladies graciously complied. There was only one hitch in the service: one of the pigeons fluttered down and sat on the music box during the reading of the First Lesson. The box started to play "Nearer, My God, to Thee" and the entire congregation stood up and joined in an encore of that grand old hymn.

The Salvation Army had little trouble in filling the big tent, for all Dawson was grateful for the presence of the sturdy young women in black bonnets who had arrived at the peak of the rush. Typhoid fever and scurvy were sweeping the town. On crude beds of spruce boughs and in overcrowded hospital corridors men now fought for their lives, as they had once fought their way over the mountains. From cabin to cabin the Army girls moved, bathing the sufferers, attending to their wants, asking no payment, but bringing medicine, care, and comfort.

On a knoll above the town stood Father Judge's hospital, where the Sisters of Sainte Anne acted as nurses. As the thin priest had anticipated, it was desperately needed in Dawson. The hospital was jammed with the sick and the dying. One of these was seventeen-year-old Bert Parker, the boy from Ontario who had come to the Klondike to strike it rich. He hadn't found any gold, but he had worked hard. He had cut wood on the creeks. He had made wages scraping mold from a shipload of bacon. Then he had started mining on a fifty-fifty basis with the owner. At this point typhoid struck him down.

Young Bert hovered between life and death all winter. The hospital was so crowded that Father Judge refused to use a bed. He slept on the floor in a hallway, with a bit of awning thrown over him. It was obvious that he, too, was dying, exhausted by his labors. But Father Judge never lost heart. "He gave hope to the sick, cheer to the dying, and he joshed the convalescents," Bert Parker wrote. One of the priest's last acts was to call the young boy to his bedside for a talk. Parker recovered, but Father Judge died.

The hospital, which stood for a half-century, was his monument. It had been built by public subscription, and almost every King on Eldorado had contributed large sums to it. For if men were prodigal in the saloons and gambling-houses, they were also openhanded in other ways. Before the summer was over, Dawson had two hospitals and three churches, all raised by public subscription. When the Presbyterian church burned down, the minister stood dejectedly looking at the embers. A group of miners quickly surrounded him. “Never mind,” they said, “we’ll build you another one.” And they did.

The Gold Rush may have brought out the worst in men, but it also brought out the best. The old sourdoughs had always lived by a strict and necessary code of honor, and now the cheechakos were learning it. It was the Golden Rule, the motto of the Yukon Order of Pioneers: “Do unto others as you would that they would do unto you.” No man starved in the Yukon as long as any man had food. Credit was unlimited. It was still an unwritten rule that a man could walk into any cabin on the trail in the owner’s absence and help himself to food and lodging for the night. In turn he must leave an adequate supply of kindling and a freshly laid fire in the stove, and he must clean up after himself.

As the gold rush whirled on to its climax, Dawson City reached its peak in population. The theaters and gambling-halls ran all night, jammed with men and women making or spending money. The streets were crowded with thousands more. Men waited in block-long queues to get their mail, for the post office facilities were overtaxed. When they could wait no longer, they paid women one dollar apiece to wait for them.

Famous men and women, and others soon to become famous, walked the streets. Arizona Charley Meadows, the western buffalo-hunter, and Captain Jack Crawford, the poet scout, both in buckskin shirts with their long silky hair hanging to their shoulders, were familiar figures on the streets. Jack London, Rex Beach, and James Oliver Curwood, all future novelists of the north, were in town. Wilson Mizner, who later owned Hollywood's famous Brown Derby restaurant, and Sid Grauman, who later founded Hollywood's famous Chinese Theatre, where movie stars leave their imprints in cement, were young men-about-town. Tex Rickard, who became the greatest fight-promoter of them all and founded Madison Square Garden in New York, was a bartender in Dawson. So was Alexander Pantages, who founded the continent's largest theater chain. Jack Kearns, who later in life became the manager of heavyweight Jack Dempsey, was a young boxer in Dawson.

The toast of Dawson that summer wasn't a gambler or a dance-hall girl, but a little nine-year-old child with golden hair named Margie Newman. She and her sisters and brothers sang and danced on the stage of the Monte Carlo, where Margie was a great hit. They called her "The Princess of the Klondike." When she sang "Annie Laurie" in her high, piping voice, or danced the Highland fling in Scottish dress, rough miners hurled nuggets onto the stage. Some even composed poetry to her. One of them wrote:

God bless you, little Margie,
For you made us better men,
God bless you, little Margie,
For you take us home again. . . .

When Margie finally left Dawson, a miner from Eldorado standing on the dock tore off his solid gold watch and nugget chain and tossed them up to her on the deck of the steamboat. Then he wrapped a hundred-dollar bill around a silver dollar and a fifty-dollar bill around another and tossed these gifts to her as well.

Out on the creeks the lucky men still washed their gold and the unlucky men wandered through the woods vainly seeking fortunes. During the starvation winter more rich claims had been staked, this time on the hills and benches that surrounded the rich Bonanza and Eldorado diggings. These hills, which were really the bottoms of ancient rivers, were worth millions. Other rich creeks had been discovered: Sulphur, Dominion, Quartz, and Last Chance. An offhand remark on a Dawson streetcorner could easily start a stampede for a spot miles away, so acute was the gold fever.

But, alas, the fever did not produce more gold. The gold that was in the Klondike had long since been spoken for, months before the men of '98 crossed the Chilkoot and swept down the river. As more and more men poured into Dawson, wages dropped and jobs became scarcer. Money still poured in from the goldfields. From June to November 1898, ten million dollars' worth of Klondike gold was sent to the United States mint in square ironbound boxes. But most of the men who stampeded to the Klondike were destitute by the winter of 1898–99. Ten thousand of them spent a hungry season, not because of lack of food this time, but because of lack of funds. The money expended in sending one hundred thousand men toward the Klondike far exceeded the amount of gold dug up that year.

It is estimated that the Klondike stampeders expended sixty million dollars in 1898 alone, or six times the total amount of gold taken from the diggings. Indeed, the total output of gold from the Yukon that year was a mere four percent of the world total. Colorado and California each exceeded the Klondike. Western Australia produced twice as much. The great Rand mine in South Africa was six times richer that year.

The Klondike certainly made many men fabulously rich. But its riches were concentrated on small parcels of ground, not spread over vast areas. It was this concentrated wealth, together with the remoteness of the country, that fired men's imaginations in 1897–98.

There were other reasons for the Klondike frenzy. The news of the discovery came at exactly the right psychological and historical moment: a depression was on, peace reigned, and adventure beckoned. Another year or so and the Spanish-American and Boer wars would have made the stampede virtually impossible. But this was at the end of the great Victorian age of exploration and expansion. Men were ripe for adventure and hungry for wealth. The Klondike provided a heaven-sent opportunity for both.

The great stampede's value lay not in the gold that men dug from the ground, but in the vast sections of the American and Canadian northwest that were opened up. Edmonton, Vancouver, and Seattle trace their subsequent prosperity directly to the Klondike. The last-named city, for example, got twenty-five millions of dollars in extra business in the winter of 1897–98. Vancouver's population almost doubled, while Edmonton sprang from a hamlet of eight hundred to a flourishing town of four thousand. The stampede had many useful by-products. Men clawing their way up the terrible Valdez Glacier found copper and stayed to mine it. Men trudging through the Peace River country found land and stayed to farm it. All of northern British Columbia was swiftly explored by the Klondikers. So were the vast lonely reaches of Alaska and the broad water highway of the Mackenzie.

There was yet another asset more intangible but no less

rewarding. The Klondike Gold Rush in many ways resembled a great war. It brutalized some men and it was the death of others, but the vast majority who survived it came out better men for the experience. Most of them were white-collar workers, soft and flabby from sedentary living. For these the Klondike stampede was its own achievement. The Chilkoot was each man's personal Everest, and in it he found triumph or defeat.

Of the one hundred thousand men involved in the stampede only four thousand found gold, and of these only the merest handful could show a profit. Yet in the scores of personal accounts that exist of this strange moment in history hardly one sounds any note of regret. The Klondike was a unique experience that few men would care to renounce. On the mountain trails men made friendships that lasted a lifetime. Men went through experiences that remained sharp and vivid for fifty years. Many of them discovered to their surprise that the actual staking of ground came as an anti-climax to the supreme drama of the trail. And others, having successfully met the challenge of the mountains and the river, didn't bother to stake at all.

As the year 1898 faded into 1899 the gold dust still continued to pour in a glittering stream onto the gold scales. On the creeks mules owned by men like Big Alec McDonald and Clarence Berry still trudged in from the mines loaded with plunder by the hundredweight. The peaceful creeks down which George Carmack and Bob Henderson had trudged two years before would never be the same again. But the great rush had spent itself. Already huge mining syndicates were consolidating blocks of claims. Men were planning new and more efficient ways of getting gold from the ground. Bedrock was being thawed by live steam instead of by slow wood fires. Soon great dredges would churn the Klondike valleys into oceans of white gravel, while giant hydraulic nozzles would tear the green hills to pieces.

Dawson still boomed on, but the seeds of its slow decline were already planted. 1898 was its finest year. In '99 the decline began.

Out from Alaska that winter seeped the news that sealed Dawson's fate. It was the same kind of news that had once emptied other mining towns, like Fortymile and Circle City. Gold had been discovered that winter on Anvil Creek at Cape Nome, Alaska. At first the news was sketchy, as it always was, and men refused to believe it, as they always did. But, skeptical or not, they began to trickle out of town in twos and threes on another long stampede two thousand miles to the new diggings. Here other men were already enduring terrible suffering in a gamble for terrible riches.

Already a tent city was springing up on Nome beach. Then in the summer of 1899 gold was discovered in large quantities in the very sands of the beach itself. The news roared across Alaska and the Yukon like a forest fire. Within a week, eight thousand people left Dawson for the new strike, as they had once left Circle City for the Klondike. Nome beach was staked for thirteen miles and mining men were estimating its output at two million dollars for the first season—more than the Klondike had produced in its initial year.

In Dawson City, log cabins could now be had for the taking, and the great Klondike Gold Rush was over as suddenly as it had begun.

AFTER . . .

IN THE YEARS THAT FOLLOWED THE GREAT STAMPEDE, the Klondike and the men who made her faded into the twilight of obscurity. For the Klondike Kings everything that followed the stampede was an anti-climax. Few of them kept for long the riches they found there. Most of them, sad to say, died penniless.

Big Alec McDonald, the richest of them all, was one of the poorest when he died. What happened to his millions? The sad fact is that Big Alec was simply too generous and too trusting. He fell for any man who had a glib tongue. He lent money to anybody who asked him for it. He backed dozens of crack-brained schemes. It got so bad that Big Alec, on being introduced to any stranger, used to ask automatically: "Are you a partner of mine?"

When his money began to drain away, Big Alec tried to repeat his former successes. He acquired more and more land on various creek beds. Alas for him, the land, more often than not, was valueless. At last his funds melted away, and he ended his life as he had begun, chopping wood and drawing water in a lonely little cabin in the wilderness.

Most of the other Klondike Kings met similar fates. Charlie Anderson, the Lucky Swede, married a pretty dance-hall singer. She had expensive tastes. He built her a castle on San Francisco Bay. But she left him shortly afterward. The rest of his wealth vanished in the great San Francisco earthquake that followed. The Lucky Swede spent the rest of his life seeking another fortune, but never found it. When he died, in 1939, he was working as a laborer in a sawmill in British Columbia.

Antone Stander married a dance-hall girl, too. Her name was Violet Raymond, and he wooed her by buying up all the diamonds in Dawson for her. Then he gave her twenty thousand dollars in gold dust and a lard pail full of nuggets. Before she left him she had taken most of his money. Stander went to work peeling potatoes on one of the ships that plied the Alaska coastal waters. He died broke in the Pioneers' Home in Sitka, Alaska. Violet fared better. When she died in 1944, she left fifty thousand dollars.

Thomas Lippy took his huge fortune back to Seattle. There he became one of the town's leading citizens. He raised money for the Y.M.C.A., which had once employed him as a clerk. He gave huge sums to charities. He took his wife around the world. His enormous fifteen-room mansion contained the finest collection of Oriental rugs in the Pacific northwest. They not only covered the floor, but hung like banners from the ceiling. But, like Big Alec, Lippy was too trusting. Obscure relatives moved into Seattle to help him spend his money. Fast-talking men pursued him to get him to back various business ventures. He put one hundred thousand dollars into each of four companies. Each of them failed. When he died in 1931 he was flat broke.

It's hard to believe, but Dick Lowe spent in a few years the six hundred thousand dollars he took out of his famous fraction. It went on riotous living. After that he slipped into obscurity. There is a last glimpse of him trying to pawn his watch in Victoria, B.C. It's believed that he died in Alaska.

As for poor Harry Ash, the bartender, he went insane. His wife killed herself.

Of all the Eldorado Kings only Clarence Berry emerges as a man of wisdom, stability, and good sense. Berry was a quiet, industrious man, married to a brave and warm-hearted woman. Berry neither drank nor gambled, but when funds were needed for a church or hospital he was always more than generous. He did not throw his money away as Dick Lowe did. He had worked hard for it, and he invested it wisely. He maintained mining interests in the Yukon and then proceeded to found a second fortune in oil in California. He died in Fresno in 1930, a wealthy and respected man.

Some men spent all or most of their lives in the Klondike and were happy to do so. Young Bert Parker found no gold, but he spent twenty-five years in the north. When he left the hospital he made a great deal of money selling newspapers. Sometimes he sold as many as a thousand papers an hour for good prices. Charlie Anderson once gave him fifty-nine dollars in gold for a single ten-cent edition. Later on the boy became an engineer.

All of his life Bert Parker remembered the great stampede. Most of his friends were men and women he'd met during the Gold Rush. Like so many others in that far-off winter of 1897–98, his whole future was changed by his decision to go north. He lived to a ripe old age and died in Vancouver, B.C. When the doctor told him he hadn't long to live, Bert Parker sat down and wrote a thorough account of what he'd seen during the stampede. Then he attended the International Convention of Sourdoughs, which is held every year on August 17—the anniversary of the discovery of gold on the

Klondike. Bert Parker was president of the convention that year, and he swore he'd live until it was over. The following week he was dead.

And what of George Carmack and his Indians, and Robert Henderson—the men who started it all?

Henderson spent most of his life roaming the Yukon valleys, searching for a new Bonanza. He never found it, but he never lost that optimism which caused him, long ago, to head up the Indian River looking for gold. One cannot help admiring this stubborn, honest prospector who, as he lay dying of cancer in Vancouver in 1933, still talked of striking it rich in British Columbia. There are men of Henderson's breed still in the north, and the country owes a great debt to them.

Carmack left Dawson moderately wealthy in the fall of 1898. He cut quite a swath in the outside world, for he was still the same bluff romantic whom the prospectors had once dubbed Lying George. He and his Indian wife, Kate, along with Skookum Jim and Tagish Charley, threw showers of nuggets from the window of a Seattle hotel. Crowds jammed the streets to catch the gold and fight for it in the gutters as Carmack laughed raucously from above. But the outside world didn't suit Kate Carmack. Once, when she lost herself in a maze of hotel corridors, she blazed a trail back to her room with a hatchet, on staircase and banister. On another occasion she and her brother were thrown into jail for drunkenness.

Finally Carmack divorced his Indian wife and married again. Kate went back to Carcross in the Yukon, where she lived out her life in moderate comfort. Tagish Charley died ignobly in a fall from the Carcross Bridge after a drinking bout. Skookum Jim, like Bob Henderson, spent the rest of his days seeking another gold mine. He trekked across the Yukon, eating sparingly and driving his massive body to the point of exhaustion. Those who remember him claim that this killed him in the end. As for Carmack, he remained moderately wealthy and died in Vancouver in the 1920s. A few paragraphs in the local papers briefly recalled that wonderful day in 1896 when he had gazed on a nugget in the waters of Rabbit Creek. But, apart from that, his passing went unnoticed.

When the Gold Rush ended, mining on the Klondike continued. In fact, it continues to this day. But the days of the individual miner, working with wheelbarrow and sluice box, did not last long. A few years after the rush, the era of the Klondike dredges began.

The whole story of these dredges is built around two strange and dramatic figures. One of them was a toothy, shaggy little man with a blond mustache. He had been a professor of Greek at Oxford University in England before he came to the Klondike with thousands of others in 1898. His name was Arthur Newton Christian Treadgold.

The other man was a strapping, heavy-jawed former prizefighter. He too came to Dawson in 1898 and went to work as a bouncer in a saloon. His name was Joseph Whiteside Boyle.

Both of these fabulous men juggled with millions. Both died broke.

Boyle got his start when he persuaded the Canadian government to grant him dredging-rights on a seven-mile chunk of the Klondike Valley. Then he proceeded to raise money and to build the biggest gold dredges in the world. Old-timers laughed at him. They said the dredges would never work. But one or two of Boyle's dredges lasted over fifty years. One ran for thirty-two seasons without a break and dug up six and a half million dollars.

A big dredge is an awe-inspiring sight. It stands three stories high and looks, on the outside, like a big, square boat. It is built in a deep pit. The pit is filled with water from the creek. The dredge floats on the surface and begins to work, digging its own pond out of the stream bed as it moves along, and as it digs, its cables and winches scream and whine like lost souls.

The dredge pivots on a sixty-foot anchor known as a "spud." The spud weighs thirty tons. The dredge sits on the spud and swings slowly from side to side. A moving belt of sharp-edged steel buckets pours endlessly out of its mouth, digging deeper and deeper into the bedrock. When it has dug deep enough, the bucket line is pulled up and the spud is yanked out of the rock. Then the dredge lurches forward about six feet on its cables; the spud is lowered and the buckets start to gnaw into the rock and gravel again. The buckets are enormous. Some of them weigh a ton and a half each, and some dredges have eighty of them.

A dredge is a sort of combination digger and floating sluice box. When the bucket chain deposits its loot inside the dredge, the coarse gravel is screened and thrown out behind. In this way are formed the tailing piles that choke the Klondike valleys. The finer sand and gold is sluiced, just as it was in the old days. It is washed down a long box containing the familiar cross bars and riffles. The heavy gold catches in the riffles; the rest of the sand washes away. The gold is finally melted and molded into bricks and shipped outside.

Joe Boyle, the man who built the big dredges, became the greatest of the Klondike Kings. At one time he owned the telephone company, power plant, laundry, sawmill, and coal mine. He sent the Dawson hockey team on a tour of North America at his own expense. When World War I came along, he dug into his pockets and outfitted an entire machine-gun battery with his own money.

Then one of the great dredges sank. Boyle went off to England to raise more money to save his company. Instead he joined the British Railway Mission to Russia and became a soldier of fortune. He wore lapel badges made of Klondike gold and he won nine medals in foreign countries. He became the confidant of queens and princes, and at one time they called him the Uncrowned King of Romania. He never returned to his bankrupt mining company on the Klondike. When the war ended, he lapsed into obscurity, to die in England, penniless, in 1923.

Meanwhile, Arthur Treadgold, the Oxford professor, had started his own company. While Boyle's dredges were churning up the Klondike, Treadgold raised money to dredge the Indian River on the other side of the divide. Then he bought up Boyle's bankrupt company and, in turn, became a Klondike King.

Treadgold didn't like the dredges which had given Joe Boyle his reputation. He wanted to find a substitute, and he squandered millions looking for one. He paid half a million dollars for two enormous land-going diggers. These fantastic machines were supposed to run on tracks and dig up the gravel as they moved. They didn't work.

Then he built a huge cableway with giant towers across one creek. A great scraper bucket was supposed to scoop up the dirt as it slid along the cable. But that wouldn't work either.

Treadgold kept spending money. He tried out various kinds of suction pumps that were supposed to suck up rocks and gravel. But none of them would work.

To this day in Dawson City you can walk along the riverbank and see lying among the mosses and willows the rusting, unused machinery that Treadgold bought.

Finally the shareholders of the company began to get restless. A series of court actions followed. In the end the wiry little Oxford professor found himself with no job. The company passed into new hands. Treadgold himself died shortly after World War II, in England. He was the last of the Klondike Kings. Like almost all the others, from Big Alec McDonald to Joe Boyle, he died broke.

The dredges still mine the Klondike and the other famous creeks. No one knows exactly how much money has come out of the area, but the sum is somewhere around three hundred million dollars. It's a pretty good guess that there's still about sixty million left.

The valleys of Bonanza and Hunker, Klondike and Eldorado bear very little resemblance to the silent, wooded watersheds that Carmack and Henderson once knew. The trees have long since gone, cut down to build cabins or provide fuel to thaw the frozen ground. Old flumes and hydraulic workings scar the hills. And everywhere, even to this day, lies the wreckage of the Gold Rush. Rusting shovels, picks, and wheelbarrows are sprinkled about the country by the thousands. Rotting sluice boxes from the old days, and crumbling cabins with ancient newspapers lining the walls, can still be found.

Abandoned boilers, winches, engines, and drills lie scattered about the land.

The little creeks no longer wind leisurely through the mosses. For each valley is now choked with enormous piles of white gravel, like endless mountain ranges. These are the tailing piles, churned up from the creek bottoms by the dredges.

But before the dredge can work at all, a heavy layer of frozen muck—as much as sixty-five feet of it—must be sliced off the surface of the valley. And after that, the gold-bearing bedrock—another ten to forty feet deep—must be completely thawed out. A dredge can't buck frost.

The result is a curious kind of mining that is unique to Alaska and the Yukon. First, bulldozers strip away all the creek-bed foliage. Then the frozen muck is torn from the ground by huge jets of water and washed away downstream and finally into the Yukon River. Giant nozzles pour out water at pressures up to one hundred twenty pounds a square inch. This is enough to tear a man to shreds, and it literally blows the soil to pieces.

Now the gravel and bedrock must be thawed so that the dredge buckets can bite into it. The early miners, of course, used wood fires. Later on steam was used. But when the timber vanished from the hills, something new had to be devised. Finally an inventor in Nome named Miles came up with an ingenious idea. Miles reasoned that water would thaw frozen gravel because cold water is still warmer than ice.

And so the company lays a vast network of pipes across each valley. And from these pipes project hoses. And from these hoses project long steel pipes with pointed ends which must be driven deep into the ground. And from each pointed end comes a jet of cold water. All summer long, day after day and week after week, water is pumped into the bowels of the earth through these thousands of pipes.

Soon the valley becomes a heaving sea of mud. The water forms an underground lake. The ground begins to heave and fall away. Hundreds of ponds appear and the earth turns to jelly. The whole land becomes a great black sponge. But by fall another chunk of ground has been thawed. The next year the dredge attacks it and the gold is claimed.

The smell of gold still hangs over Dawson City. The streets are literally paved with gold. During the depression of the thirties a great many unemployed men went to the Klondike seeking work. While they waited for jobs, they began to dig up the earth and gravel which lay under the creaking old board sidewalks. Sure enough, there was gold there, fine dust that could be panned. It had filtered down from the pockets of thousands of men who had walked these streets in the days of 1898.

One day the owner of the theater where little Margie

Newman once sang decided to put in a new floor. While the carpenters were tearing up the old one, he panned the earth underneath. In two and a half hours he got fifteen hundred dollars. Some of the nuggets, obviously, had never reached the stage.

At its height, Dawson City had a population of 35,000 but the stampede of 1898 died out almost as quickly as it began. For years Dawson City was almost a ghost town. Today, about 2,000 full-time residents live in Dawson City but the population swells to 60,000 when the tourists arrive in the summer.

Visitors step aboard the Klondike Spirit for a taste of travel on an old paddle wheel steamer or stroll down wooden walkways in town. Some of the old landmarks like the Palace Grand Theatre have been reconstructed and many sites have been designated of National Historic significance by the Canadian government. The Canadian Imperial Bank of Commerce is still open and gold is still weighed and handled there.

Placer mining to recover gold takes place on nearby creeks and rivers. Remnants of dredges can be seen throughout the Klondike but the No. 4 Dredge is only ten miles out of Dawson City. It is the biggest wooden hull, bucket-line gold dredge in North America. It rests on Claim No. 17 on Bonanza Creek and is now maintained by Parks Canada.

You can still pan for gold in Dawson City and visitors enjoy many events including the celebration of its greatest holiday,

August 17, the anniversary of the discovery of gold on Bonanza Creek.

Jack London's cabin attracts many fans but perhaps the most interesting building in Dawson today is a little sod-roofed log cabin tucked under the hill, with a pair of moose antlers over the door. This is the place where every tourist wants to be taken. For it was here that Robert W. Service, the Bard of the Yukon, wrote his famous Klondike poems.

Service's two most famous poems are "The Shooting of Dan McGrew" and "The Cremation of Sam McGee." Largely because of these, which appeared in a book called *Songs of a Sourdough,* Service became a rich man. Indeed, he made more money than all but a handful of men who rushed to the Klondike seeking gold.

All this is the more strange because Service had never seen the Klondike when he wrote these two poems. Nor did he ever witness the Klondike Gold Rush. He was a young bank clerk who went north to the Yukon in 1905. He went not to Dawson, but to Whitehorse, four hundred miles to the southwest. And here he wrote the verses that made him famous. The following year, 1906, eight years after the great stampede, Service arrived in the Klondike. He spent only a few years there, but his cabin has been visited by thousands of men and women.

Service left Dawson before World War I, and never returned. He spent his life in France, far from the scene of the stampede. Unlike the men who inspired his verses, Service invested his money wisely. He deserved his wealth, for nobody ever captured the spirit of those far-off days of '98 better than this shy little bank clerk who wrote:

This is the Law of the Yukon, that only the Strong shall thrive;
That surely the Weak shall perish, and only the Fit survive.
Dissolute, damned and despairful, crippled and palsied and slain,
This is the Will of the Yukon—lo, how she makes it plain!

Index

Alaska Commercial Company, 11, 36, 54, 62, 75, 80, 118
Alaska Highway, 103
Alaska Territory, gold discovered in, 2
Alice (steamboat), 75
All-Canadian route, 101–3
Allen, Eugene, 122
Amur (steamboat), 63
Anderson, Charley "Lucky Swede," 38, 141
Arctic Ocean, 105
Ash, Harry, 45, 54, 90, 142
Ashcroft, British Columbia, 100
Athabasca Landing, 104
Athabaska River, 104–5
Avonmore, Lord, 102

Bank of British North America, 50
Beach, Rex, 133
Bella (steamboat), 54, 56, 58, 75, 78, 79
Bell River, 108
Berry, Clarence, 37, 40, 41, 51, 137, 142–43
Boer War, 136
Bompas, Bishop William, 7–8
Bonanza Creek, 34–36, 40–41, 46, 134
Booth, Edwin, 53

Boyle, Joseph Whiteside, 146, 147–48
Bristol (steamboat), 63
British Columbia:
  Ashcroft route, 100
  exploration of, 136
  routes to Klondike in, 99–100
British Columbia:
  Stikine River route, 100–101
Bruceth, Fred, 35–36

California Gold Rush (1849), 23, 59
Cape Nome, Alaska, gold discovered in, 138–39
Carmack, George Washington, 17–18, 138
  claims staked by, 28, 31, 32
  and gold discovery, 27–28, 42, 53
  later life of, 144–45
  as Lying George, 23, 32
  meeting with Henderson, 22–30
  as mystic, 23–24
  publicizing his discovery, 31–33
  at Rabbit Creek, 25–27
  as Siwash/Stick George, 22–23
Carmack, Kate, 22, 144–45
Carroll, Jim, 92
Charles Hamilton (steamboat), 75
Cheechakos (newcomers), 34
Chicago, spiritualists in, 65
Chilkoot Pass, 68, 83–88, 90–96
  Canyon City, 84
  Carmack on, 23
  disasters on, 95–96
  Dyea Trail, 84, 85–86, 90, 92
  at Lake Lindemann, 109
  photographs of, 86, 90
  Pleasant Camp, 84
  The Scales, 86, 87, 91

Sheep Camp, 84–85, 87
stories of, 89–96
at the summit, 87
Chisholm, Tom, 125
Circle City, Yukon Territory, 8–11
gold stampede out of, 45, 53
isolation of, 44
miners' meetings in, 13–15
murder case in, 14–15
thefts in, 15–16, 78–79
Constantine, Capt. Charles, 78
Crawford, Capt. Jack, 133
"Cremation of Sam McGee, The" (Service), 154
Curwood, James Oliver, 133

Davis, Sergeant Major, 78
Dawson City, Yukon Territory, 33
changes in, 122, 128–29, 132–33, 135
code of honor in, 132
currency in, 126–27
decline of, 138
disease in, 126
flood danger in, 120, 122
food shortages in, 51–52, 74–82
Front Street in, 124–25
hospital in, 45, 131, 153
iced in, 80–82, 97, 99, 108, 122
isolation of, 51
laws upheld in, 127–28
"lay" arrangement in, 48–49
major routes to, 98–99
money in, 50, 53
new arrivals in, 52–53, 74, 119, 120–22, 123–24, 128–29
population of, 47, 55, 74, 123, 132, 152

Dawson City, Yukon Territory (*cont.*)
steamboats to and from, 54–55, 56–59, 74–76, 78, 97, 122, 128
stories about, 125–28
streets paved with gold, 151
tourism in, 129–30, 152–53
Dempsey, Jack, 133
Destruction City, 107
Dick Lowe Fraction, 47
Duck, The, 103
Dyea, Alaska, as gateway to Chilkoot Pass, 68, 81, 83, 84
Dyea Trail, 84, 85–86, 90, 92

Edmonton, Canada, 102, 136
Edmonton route:
All-Canadian route via, 101–3
to Dawson via, 99
Eldorado Creek, 36, 38, 40–41, 46, 48, 134
Excelsior (steamboat), 57, 58, 62

Father of the Yukon (McQuesten), 11
Fawcett, Thomas, 78
Five Finger Rapids, 118
Fort Reliance, 11
Fort Simpson, 105
Forty Liars, The, 7
Fortymile, Yukon Territory, 2, 3–8
customs in, 5–6
gold stampedes out of, 31–33
how to get to, 3
people of, 6, 33
Fort Yukon, 75–76, 79, 80

Gandolfo, Signor, 124
Garland, Hamlin, 91

Gates, Swiftwater Bill, 48
Glenora, British Columbia, 100–101
Goddard, Capt. A. J., 90
Gold Bottom Creek, 21, 24–25, 29, 30, 31, 41–43
Grand Forks, Canada, 27
Grauman, Sid, 133

Hamilton, Charles, 77
Hansen, Capt. J. E., 75–76, 78
Hawthorne, Mont, 91
Healy, Capt. John J., 76–77
Hegg, E. A., 90
Heming, Arthur, 101, 105
Henderson, Robert, 17–30, 138
  at Gold Bottom, 21, 24–25, 29, 30, 31, 41, 42
  later life of, 144
  lost opportunity of, 26, 30, 43
  meeting with Carmack, 22–30
  misfortunes of, 41–43
  prejudice against Indians, 24, 26
  and Yukon Order of Pioneers, 21, 24, 43
Hitchcock, Mary E., 129–30
Hootalinqua, Yukon Territory, 117–18
Hudson's Bay Company, 104, 105, 118
Hunker, Andrew, 42–43
Hunker Creek, 43
Huson, Billy, 89–90

Indian River, 19–21
International Convention of Sourdoughs, 143–44
Islander (steamboat), 63

John J. Healy (steamboat), 75, 77
Johns, William, 35–36
Johnson, Cutthroat, 10

Judge, Father William, 45–46, 131

Kearns, Jack, 133
King of the Klondike (McDonald), 39
Klondike City, Yukon Territory, as Lousetown, 52
Klondike Gold Rush:
  and end of depression, 61, 136
  legacy of, 136–37
  mining syndicates in, 138
  reasons for, 136
  stampede of, 61–67, 135
  start of, 18, 31, 55
  syndicates to exploit, 65–66
  tall tales and legends of, 60, 137
  wreckage of, 149–50
Klondike River, 6, 22
  dredging on, 145–51
  surveys of, 46–47
  as "Thronduick," 17–18
Kronstadt, Jim, 14

Ladue, Joseph, 19–21, 32, 33, 52, 58, 60–61
Lake Bennett:
  boat-building on, 110–12
  difficulty of getting to, 73
  at end of White Pass, 109
  at head of Yukon River, 71, 96, 109
  leaving for Dawson, 113–14
  rapids out of, 112–13
Lake Lindemann, 96, 109
Lesser Slave Lake, 104
Linville, Tom, 92
Lippy, Thomas, 39, 58, 60, 142
London, Jack, 90–91, 133
Loucheaux Indians, 8
Lowe, Dick, 47, 142

MacCaley, Norman, 116
MacDonald, Archdeacon, 8
Mackenzie River, 99, 101–3, 105–6, 136
Margaret (steamboat), 75
Mayo, Al, 11
McDonald, Big Alec, 39, 49–51, 129, 137, 140–41
McPhee, Bill, 31
McQuesten, Napoleon LeRoy "Jack," 10–13
Meadows, Arizona Charley, 133
Miles (inventor), 150–51
Miles Canyon, 115–17
miners' meetings, 13–15
Mizner, Wilson, 133
Moore, Billy, 69

Newman, Margie, 133–34, 151–52
Ning Chow (steamboat), 64
North American Trading and Transportation Company, 75, 76
Northwest Mounted Police "Mounties":
- customs duties paid to, 115
- guarding the border, 70, 72
- at Lake Bennett, 111–12
- at Tagish Lake, 115, 122
- upholding the law, 127–28

Oatley, Lottie and Polly, 125
Ogilvie, William, 46–47, 51, 52

Palmer, Frederick, 91
Pantages, Alexander, 133
Parker, Bert:
- arrival at Dawson City, 119
- at Lake Bennett, 113–14
- later life of, 143–44
- starting out, 64

Parker, Bert (*cont.*)
as typhoid sufferer, 131
on White Pass, 88–89, 93–94
Peace River:
farmland along, 103–4, 136
route to Dawson via, 99, 103
Peel River, 106
Portland (steamboat), 57, 59, 61, 62
Portus B. Weare (steamboat), 56, 57, 75, 78, 79
Preacher's Creek, 8–9

Rabbit Creek, 25–27, 29, 31
name changed to Bonanza, 34, 41
Rat River, tracking along, 106–7
Raymond, Violet, 141
Reid, Frank, 95
Rhodes, Louis, 34–35, 40, 58
Rickard, Tex, 133

Salvation Army, 130
San Francisco:
earthquake in, 141
gold stampede out of, 62
Klondike gold arriving in, 58–60
steamboat traffic to and from, 57–58
Scurvy, 107–8
Seattle:
gold stampede out of, 62
Klondike gold arriving in, 59–60
prosperity in, 136
steamboat traffic to and from, 57
Service, Robert W., 154–55
"Shooting of Dan McGrew, The" (Service), 154
Sisters of Sainte Anne, 131
Sitting Bull, Chief, 122
Siwash Indians, 22–24, 117–18
Sixtymile River, 19

Skagway, Alaska, 68–73
as gateway to White Pass, 68, 81
lawlessness in, 69
Skagway Trail, 72–73, 88, 92
Skeena River, 100, 118
Skeena swamp, 100
Skookum Jim, 22, 24, 27, 28, 31, 144, 145
Slavin, Frank, 125
Smith, Jefferson Randolph "Soapy," 94–95
Smith, Texas, 103
Snow, George, 53
Snow, Monte, 53–54
Songs of a Sourdough (Service), 154–55
Sourdoughs, 4–5
Spanish-American War, 136
Squaw Rapids, 116
Stander, Antone, 36–37, 141
Stanley, "Papa" William, 61
Steffens, Lincoln, 60
Stick Indians, 22–24, 117–18
Stikine River, 100–101, 118

Tacoma, Washington, gold rush associations in, 65
Tagish Charley, 22, 28, 31, 144, 145
Tagish Lake, 114–15, 122
Teslin Lake:
interior route to Dawson via, 98–99, 101
and Yukon River, 117–18
Thirtymile River, 117
Trail of Ninety-Eight, 98
Treadgold, Arthur Newton Christian, 145, 148–49

Valdez Glacier, 136
Van Buren, Edith, 129–30
Vancouver, British Columbia, 101, 136
Victoria, British Columbia, 101

Walden, Arthur Treadwell, 44–45, 92

Walsh, Commissioner, 121–22
Washburn, Jim, 14
Weare, Ely, 77
Weare, Portus B., 66
Western Union, 100
Whitehorse Rapids, 116
White Pass, 68, 70–73
  difficulties of, 72–73, 81, 89
  at Lake Bennett, 109
  Skagway Trail, 72–73, 88, 92
  stories of, 88–89, 93–94
Williamette (steamboat), 63–64
Williams (prospector), 1–2
Wind City, 107–8
Wind River, 106, 107
Wrangell, Alaska, 100

Yukon Order of Pioneers, 21, 24, 43, 132, 153
Yukon River, 3, 44
  Lake Bennett at head of, 71, 96, 109
  and Miles Canyon rapids, 115–17
  water trail to the Klondike, 98, 117–18
Yukon Territory:
  difficult life in, 5–6
  gold discovered in, 2, 9, 44
  mountain passes to, 68
  place-mining in, 37–38

Zarnowsky, John, 39

ABOUT THE AUTHOR

Award-winning Canadian author PIERRE BERTON grew up in Dawson amid the debris of the gold stampede. His parents had moved to the Yukon for the 1898 Gold Rush and he spent his teens working in Klondike mining camps listening to first-hand accounts of strange adventures.

Berton became a master storyteller himself. He was the youngest city editor of a daily Canadian newspaper at age twenty-one and became a television personality as well as a journalist. He wrote fifty books including the bestselling adult book *Klondike: The Last Great Gold Rush,* and received over thirty literary awards including the Governor General's Award for Creative Non-Fiction (three times), and the Stephen Leacock Medal of Humour.

BOOKS IN THIS SERIES

Abraham Lincoln: Friend of the People
BY CLARA INGRAM JUDSON

Admiral Richard Byrd: Alone in the Antarctic
BY PAUL RINK

Alexander the Great
BY JOHN GUNTHER

Amelia Earhart: Flying Solo
BY JOHN BURKE

The Barbary Pirates
BY C. S. FORESTER

Battle in the Arctic Seas
BY THEODORE TAYLOR

Behind Enemy Lines: A Young Pilot's Story
BY H. R. DEMALLIE

Ben Franklin: Inventing America
BY THOMAS FLEMING

Daniel Boone: The Opening of the Wilderness
BY JOHN MASON BROWN

General George Patton: Old Blood and Guts
BY ALDEN HATCH

George Washington: Frontier Colonel
BY STERLING NORTH

Geronimo: Wolf of the Warpath
BY RALPH MOODY

Invasion: The Story of D-Day
BY BRUCE BLIVEN, JR.